The Heart is a Noisy Room

The Heart is a Noisy Room

Your inner voices, why
they matter – and how
to win them over

Dr Ronald Boyd-MacMillan

HODDER

First published in Great Britain in 2018 by Hodder & Stoughton
An Hachette UK company

This paperback edition first published in 2019

1

Unless indicated otherwise, Scripture quotations are taken from the
Holy Bible, New Living Translation (NLT), copyright © 1996, 2004,
2015 by Tyndale House Foundation. All rights reserved.

A CIP catalogue record for this title is available from the British Library

ISBN 978 1 473 67715 9
eBook ISBN 978 1 473 67716 6

Typeset in Adobe Garamond by Hewer Text UK Ltd, Edinburgh
Printed and bound in Great Britain by Clays Ltd, Elcograf S.p.A.

Hodder & Stoughton policy is to use papers that are natural, renewable
and recyclable products and made from wood grown in sustainable
forests. Th e logging and manufacturing processes are expected to
conform to the environmental regulations of the country of origin.

Hodder & Stoughton Ltd
Carmelite House
50 Victoria Embankment
London EC4Y 0DZ

www.hodderfaith.com

*For Eolene – who gives me the best vision
of God I could ever wish for*

Keep your heart with all vigilance;
for from it flow the springs of life.

Proverbs 4:23 ESV

In a lifetime as a Spiritual Director one constant tragedy stands out ... that most
Christians catastrophically fail to rate their own experience of God. Yet everyone
has received a treasure beyond price. Fr William Broderick

Contents

1

The Heart as a Noisy Room Full of Voices

THIS IS NOT your usual Christian book. I'll start with a confession: I struggle to read most Christian books anymore. I'm busy, and I get irritated with books that start with cringing personal stories which go on so long it's thirty pages before you get a sniff of the point. Then, after you get this hint, you have to wade through a couple of hundred pages of worthy padding, bug-eyed stories, a fund of testimonies, and promises of wholeness, fullness and power to rival Jesus himself.

This is not that kind of book.

These next few pages – with the minimum of testimony and story – share what this book is about. Take your shot at it now. Don't waste your time. Decide now whether it's worth the price of perseverance or not.

It's about our voices. What they are doing to us. What they are taking away from us. What they can give to us . . . if we know how to deal with them.

It starts with this: our heart is a noisy room **full of voices**. It's a party in there. You can hear the pop of corks, shouts, laughter and dialogue. Some voices are raised in anger. Some voices are sad. From a distance it is hard to distinguish. But the heart is the place from which all our controlling voices emanate, where our essential inner dialogues occur, where our self-consciousness reverberates. That self-consciousness is what makes us unique as humans. Or at least, dolphins – if they have self-consciousness – haven't written any books about it yet. Your heart, my heart, everyone's heart, is a noisy room full of voices. These voices can come deep from childhood, or from our culture, or from habits embraced in adulthood. Some even come from God, and some from the very pit of hell. The ones we immediately remember tend to be negative:

'I'm no good.'

'I've missed my chance . . . I'll never make it now.'

'I wish I was more like her, but I'll never be because I'm stupid/ugly.'

'You're doomed to fail . . . you've always messed up.'

But voices can also take positive forms:

'Things are sure to get better.'

'Come on, you can be the best in the world at this.'

'I will prevail because I'm special.'

'I will leave a great legacy.'

OK so far? These voices are essentially strings of sentences recurring in our heads that seem to have a distinct personality that 'monologue' to us, sometimes so fast we just feel them rather than hear the words spelled out. These voices are asking us to adopt a certain perspective on life.

You are not weird because you have them. Most people have them. They are normal. What might be a bit weird is if you hear them audibly, a lot, and feel you have to do what they want. But that is very rare, and not always a sign of schizophrenia.

These voices run our lives. Our heart is a debating chamber that runs our lives. Our inner dialogues determine whether or not we will fulfil our dreams, keep us sane or not, enable us to enjoy God . . . or not. They are the arena where our deepest desires meet our conscious intentions, and these voices – and how we respond to them – either cramp or create a life of fullness. Although these voices are not who we are, they try to take over who we are . . . and frequently succeed. They are persistent, permanent and powerful enough to lay down rails upon which we run our lives.

These voices generally ruin our lives. Our voices usually try to tear us away from our deepest identity in God. It's easy to see how negative voices ruin us. Take a harsh parental voice that has left you with the voice, 'That's not good enough.' So no matter what you achieve (and people with this voice usually achieve a lot), the voice robs you of all joy from it.

Yet even positive voices can have the same ruinous effect. I knew someone who had a strong voice that essentially was, 'I will be the best doctor in the world.' Sounds marvellous. Sounds altruistic. Sounds Christian even. But only when you forget that your deepest identity is to enjoy God, not to have a profession. This man had substituted an achievement addiction for knowing God. When he contracted a disease that meant he could no longer perform surgery, he went to pieces. He had lost his identity, but he had lost a false one, not a true one. It took him years to prove the truth of an old

Celtic saying: When the false gods go out, the true God comes in.

Most catastrophically, these voices prevent us from experiencing God with the fullness we deserve and the fullness God desires. Because they are located in the heart, they are well placed to rob us of our intimacy with God. Intimacy is a heart-to-heart knowing, and when it comes to God, that intimacy takes a unique form. He is actually resident within our heart, but his voice is not inclined to shout. *The fact is, we are creatures who say we want a heart-to-heart meeting with God, yet will do everything in our power to avoid it.* Why? Probably because if you go into the heart and meet your voices, you are going to meet three people – the person you really are (ugly); a devil who hates you (nasty) and God, your maker, who knows absolutely everything about you (fearful). That's scary.

So scary most people don't go there. Maya Angelou said that most people don't grow up, they just grow older. Even if you have the courage and desire to break the unconscious power of these voices, where's the door? What is the door to the noisy room? It's the very opposite of what keeps us away from the room of the heart. Busyness keeps us on the superficial level of life. Stillness takes us deep. Stillness is the door. It doesn't still the voices. It just enables us to hear the voices all the more clearly: no longer a babble. We have to still the other voices to listen. Most of us don't know how! It's fascinating that one of the most popular therapies for dealing with our voices today is mindfulness-based cognitive behavioural therapy (MCBT), a so-called third wave of treatments that seek to use stillness to negate the clamour of the voices.

Most vitally, these voices contain terrible lies, and they do not represent who we are. We are not the same as our voices . . . however much we may think we are. You are not that terrible person when a parent or guardian screamed, 'YOU'RE DEFECTIVE!' No, you are not. Or when they crooned, 'You're my perfect little angel.' Nor are you perfect. But the danger is we fuse our self to the voices, because we lack the confidence and self-knowledge to know the difference. Relax. You are not the same person as the voices inside you, however much they pretend you are!

Most delightfully, if we face our voices, they can also save us. Our voices are not something we can get rid of. They are too deep. You might as well tear out your heart. But if handled correctly, our voices can actually provide guidance. They turn from terrorists to avatars, and show us the way to be whole and, ultimately, the way to an enjoyment of God. I'm going to propose five ways to interact with our voices so that they no longer ruin us, but rather assist us in our renewal. Keep going on automatic pilot with these voices, and your identity will be shrunk down to their noisy, warring fragments of selfhood. Confront them, befriend them, ask God to defang them, relativise them, and even surround them with a culture of contradiction, and you will win – win through to a larger, better person. After all, there are seven billion people on the planet, but only you can be you.

Most frighteningly, our voices are hardly ever talked about. You'll never hear a sermon about them. There are few Christian books about them. A strand of self-help literature foolishly pretends to fix them. They usually concentrate on the negative voices and expect you to come up with the strength to see them off. Wrong strategy. You might as well try to sink an ocean liner with a pea shooter. The voices will win every time. We can't get rid of them. But we can shrink them, or even use them. Sure, the world of psychology has some insights. There is an emphasis on 'self-talk tapes' that can reprogram us, and a whole new school of treatment – CBT – has evolved to assist with the fight. Help us it does, especially the so-called third wave of CBT, which adds mindfulness into the mix, a form of stilling and detaching from the power of the voices rather than trying to alter their content. But this is mostly technique, like removing the chemical dependence of alcoholism, without providing the meaning or impetus to fill a life of sobriety. Here we are talking about the goal of life, which is to enjoy God, and our voices are – until we know how to handle them – out to offer a false identity in anything else but God. Ultimately, we do not have the resources in ourselves to deal with our voices. The goal is not merely to manage our voices, but use them to transform our lives . . . in a Godward direction.

Fabulous verse this: Isaiah 30:21, which in the NIV reads, 'Whether you turn to the right or to the left, your ears will hear a voice behind you, saying, "This is the way; walk in it."' God's voice called Israel to return to their primary identity – to be a distinct people in his image, and show the world the love of God. Be who I made you to be, says God.

That's what the voice of God does, should you hear it in the neighbourhood of your noisy heart. It's an invitation to go back to your primary identity, one where there is a balance between being and doing, not just being. Where you live out your uniqueness, and your living is an overflow of the love you feel from your Creator.

So that's what this book is all about. Simple, but massively complex, the more so because it's a subject rarely treated. Your mind is full of voices. You have a running dialogue with the universe. You have a subtext running like a ticker tape across the bottom of your vision. Like it or not, they are running your life. Face it – they are probably ruining your life. But what do you do? Hold on to the key idea which drives this book – *those voices that are ruining your life are also the same voices that will save your life . . . if you know how to deal with them!*

So be careful if you want to keep reading. Here is your warning: your inner dialogue will never be the same again!

Was that a promise of transformation that snuck in there? I'm not sure what the promise is. I'm just not one of those Christians who 'count it all joy'. I have found the Christian life a struggle, but a worthwhile one. The face of God comes and goes, and most of the time I have to push myself to see his face in the rain at sunset, or the wind rustling through trees. In fact, maybe God is so everywhere it looks like he is nowhere, if you can keep track with that. Of course, if you are the type of person who gets seven resurrections before breakfast, this book is not for you. You shouldn't be reading any books at all. But I do find the Christian life epic after a fashion. It's a drama of love, crucifixion, emptiness, weakness, grief, passion and joy that I choose to experience on a daily basis. But the drama is often disguised. It's a drama that does not look like a drama, especially not the Hollywood version. More like an Andrei Tarkovsky film than a Stephen

Spielberg. Tarkovsky was famous for holding his film shots of ruins, forest or fire until you grew bored, and then you got this magical moment when you saw afresh, and wonder was renewed at the spiritual in the ordinary. It takes a certain kind of eye to see it. And a disciplined patience. It's not easy. Not always fabulous. But always, in a way, *filling* enough of reality to make it the best kind of way to get through this world as we find it.

As for your voices, yes, most of them will always be there. You can't get rid of them on the whole. But you can definitely turn around from being invisibly dominated to being helpfully guided by them.

And that could save your life.

Or give you a new one.

Or, at least, a better one.

2

What is a Voice Anyway?

OK, WHAT IS a voice? Where might it come from? Why is it so powerful? How might we say it actually has the power to run our lives?

When I first started teaching on this, this was my first pass on the subject. I defined a voice this way: **'A voice is a persistent, powerful message, from yourself to yourself, that prevents and keeps you from embracing your true self.'**

The idea here was to show these things through the elements of this definition:

Persistent. It's part of your identity. It feels familiar. Even if it is never named, it is a companion over time.

Powerful. We tend to believe it. We rarely question its truth, and we have an emotion every time the voice goes off.

Message. It's a declaration or assertion, emerging from the subconscious in most cases. It's asking us to take a point of view – I am rubbish, or, I am invincible.

From yourself to yourself. The voice is within, internal, rarely spoken out, but you often find yourself in dialogue with it.

Prevents and keeps. These voices are trying to prevent you from getting what you really need more deeply. They are substitutes of lesser identities for who you really are.

True self. Our deepest identity is to love, know and serve God, right? Every Christian affirms that, at least theoretically. According to the book of Genesis, we are placed into a paradise garden and given three gifts: *Something to enjoy*: 'You may freely eat the fruit of every tree in the garden' (Genesis 2:16); *something to do*: 'Tend and watch over it' (Genesis 2:15), and, *something to avoid*: 'Don't eat of the tree of the knowledge of good and evil' (Genesis 2:17). Yes, even paradise is dangerous. In this great fellowship garden that is the world, we are to make our way through it in this way, and that is what a voice does not want us to do. It wants to create a self-dependence, or over-rate the *something to do* element, so we get defined by our achievements, and that makes it impossible to sit and enjoy God. It's our true self that is the target for the voices. St Ignatius's first principle sums it up well: we are from love, for love, of love. If that gets into your core, life can be lived aright.

So that was the first pass. But as I kept thinking and talking about it, there were two slight problems with this. One was, not all voices come from ourselves to ourselves. As a description of the *arena* of the voices, fair enough, because the main reverberation of the voices is internal; but as a description of the *origins* of the voices, it's inadequate. Most voices probably do come from ourselves, but since we are people who believe in the sacred, there are two other sources of the voices that are quite external to us – God and the pit. Whether you take the devil metaphorically or not, evil does seem to have been allotted the power to suggest, and to take those suggestions into our very hearts. Jesus famously duels with the devil in the wilderness, and although we are not told what form the devil's voices took, the least we can infer is that they entered Jesus' consciousness, whether or not the devil was sitting on a rock with a tail and antlers, red from sunburn.

But there was another problem with my first definition. It didn't really describe what a voice was like.

So here's my second pass: **'If you have (A) streams of sentences in your head, (B) that recur frequently, (C) which seem to have a distinct perspective, (D) and that carry an emotional feeling with them, you've got Voices.'**

Yep, that's a more technical definition of what a voice actually is. It's important to see what a voice is not. It does not have to be:

- audible
- loud
- overwhelming
- sacred-sounding.

Nor does it have to come using a particular pronoun, like 'You' or 'I'. Nor does the voice have to be experienced as a particular mini-person, and indeed some good research shows that the voice can form without extensive sentence streams, as our brains can use shorthand to convey the perspective. Martin Laird, in his beautiful book *A Sunlit Absence*, has a chapter called 'Our Collection of Videos', and he defines them as:

> . . . inner chatter . . . something like a video that constantly plays in the mind only to be rewound and played again and again and again. For some it might be a predominantly visual sequence of distractions, for others predominantly aural, or a combination of both. The insidious thing about these videos is that they have a way of cultivating a psychological identification with them.[1]

What he's calling our videos I suppose I am calling our voices. But put in these ways, most of us have them. **In fact, we'd be a bit weird if we didn't**.

So much for the technical, I hear you yawn. It's the actual power I want to talk about, and it is my view that these voices are trying to shape our identities, and the less attention we pay to them, the more our personality is shaped wrongly. If we pay attention to them correctly, we have a chance of being the person God wants us to be. They are trying to label us. *It feels like a person is inside us that isn't us.* These labels matter. 'You are a waste of space', 'Shut up, you've nothing to offer', 'You will always be defective'.

Feel the power?

---

[1] Martin Laird, *A Sunlit Absence: Silence, Awareness, and Contemplation* (Oxford: Oxford University Press, 2011), p.25.

OK, a bit abstract? Let's fix that! Look out: personal stories alert. Let's get a sense of what a voice sounds like and the power it has.

Recently I concluded ten trips around China, visiting over two hundred churches, a few Catholic ones, but mostly Protestant churches, from the underground house churches to the above-ground Three Self Patriotic Movement. And in all corners of this grand country – from Harbin in the north, to Urumqi in the far west, to Hainan and Kunming in the south, and all along the great coastal cities of Fuzhou, Shanghai, Hankou and Qingdao – after a while I began to notice something about the preaching. It didn't matter what tradition, whether Catholic or Protestant, whether official or unofficial. The sermons were all the same in this respect – *they all contained exhaustive lists on how to be worthy of God*. It seemed this was the church of thousand and one commandments. Yes, the gospel was in there. Yes, the Scriptures were honoured. Yes, the people were faithful and the preachers were trying their best. But the net result was for the worshipper to leave the church weighed down with a burden of guilt and feeling that they had to try a lot harder in order to deserve God's blessings.

I was reticent to share this impression, but one day when we were visiting Chengdu I met another great China watcher. I knew her well and gave her my impressions. To my surprise she said, 'Well, of course that's how we preach, because that's due to the *voice we hear from our parents growing up.*'

She said, 'You've got to understand how a typical Chinese

family works. I know; I was raised in one. From years one to seven, you are a spoiled child. You can do practically nothing wrong. But then something happens around age five, six or seven. Something changes, and *you have to perform*. Suddenly, you have to get As at school, or your parents will be displeased. If you don't get great grades, you are disgracing the family. And your parents are saying to you through their words and actions in a way that takes the form of a powerful internal voice, "We will only love you if you come top of the class." You wake to a new world. In the old one love was offered unconditionally. In the new world it becomes conditional: "Make the grade and you are worthy to receive our love!"

'That voice then permeates everything, and gets transposed out, so that God becomes a version of a demanding Chinese parent. He doesn't really love us unconditionally. We'd better shape up, get holy, and only then will his love flow towards us.'

No wonder I'd staggered out of those meetings crushed with guilt. And hark at the power of it. Millions of Chinese Christians perhaps losing their grip on the big thing that makes Christianity unique among the world religions: *grace*. We don't have to earn the favour of God. That's the way of the Pharisee. Jesus taught differently, but the voice got in the way. The voice that had come from Confucian duty, and parental pressure.

Hmmn. It did ring a bell even in my own culture, which was far away from China. I was attending a Bible study with a Scottish gentleman. A very nice man: good husband, faithful father, committed at church, a real salt-of-the-earth type.

But I began to notice something (and of course, this is always easier to notice in someone else): whatever Scripture we were studying, he always had the exact same reaction to it – guilt! Guilt that he wasn't trying hard enough to please God. Guilt that he wasn't dedicated enough to God. Guilt that he was being too soft on himself, and working his own spiritual ruin.

Now, it didn't come out in such bald terms. That's a diagnosis. It would show up more subtly. Once, we were talking about the verse, 'Let the word of God dwell in you richly.' Cue this man and he would start to say, with a defeated air, 'My, I just don't give enough time to my Bible. It's terrible. I try to make the time, but I don't succeed well enough. I must set my alarm tomorrow for half past five and make a start again.' And he would leave the Bible study – as I'm sure he left church every week – with an exhausting task list of things he must try harder at to please God.

Now there's a voice driving that. It's called, for want of a better term, 'Undeserving Voice'. I know exactly where it comes from – it comes from a particular type of Scottish upbringing. I remember the day when I won a spelling competition in primary school. Quite an achievement, I may say, even though I don't think we had any Einsteins at the primary school I was attending. I ran all the way home in great excitement and showed it to my mother. She smiled, but added, 'Dinna go get'n a big heid.' That's broad Scots for 'Don't go getting a big head'.

A little crestfallen at this muted reaction, I ventured to point out what a singular, world-beating honour this was.

She was moved to add, 'Who do think you are? Just suffer the word of exhortation.' Stern rebukes always came in the language of the King James Version. Now, my mother wasn't being ungracious. She loved me, but she was Scottish of a certain generation, wary of all notions of pride, where all celebration was premature celebration. She just wanted to keep me from getting above my station. But when that notion gets glued on to a church theology where no one deserves grace, and everyone is falling short, you end up with an embedded 'Undeserving Voice' that intrudes even on your very intimate times with God.

Say you are reading Isaiah 49:16, where God is saying, 'See, I have written your name on the palm of my hands' and you just begin to take that in when Undeserving Voice pops up to say, 'Hey, that's God speaking to Israel, not you. Don't get ahead of yourself.' Or you are reading the annunciation passage, and the angel Gabriel says to Mary, 'Greetings, favoured woman.' In *The Message* paraphrase the sense of it is caught really well: 'Good morning, you're beautiful with God's beauty. Beautiful inside and out! God be with you.' Ah, what a message. So you start to think, 'Wow, I'm as beautiful as Mary in the sight of God. We're all equally valuable in God's sight.' And just as you set yourself to receive that compliment from God, Underserving Voice pops up and says, 'Wait a minute. You're no Mary. She was pure. You've got a few things on your conscience, haven't you?' And that compliment from God to you, that you are favoured, you are beautiful, gets snatched away. Undeserving Voice won't let you receive it.

And that's just the way one single voice snatches our joy, or hurts a culture, or rips the heart out of the gospel in a church experiencing the world's largest revival in the history of Christendom. The church of a thousand and one commandments.

Voices. They matter. They matter an awful lot.

3

How Voices Worked in Me

So we are learning what voices are. And how powerful they can be. But more needs to be said about that, and we need to start offering a bit of hope too, as to how we can find our way through them to become a fuller, more joyful person. After that, we'll move on to the business of how you can identify your voices and the role they are playing in your life.

So it's time to get a lot more personal. I must come clean and explain what brought me to an interest in this in the first place.

I began to think about this on a retreat when I was in my early forties. I was no spring chicken in the faith, and I suppose I was going along because I had found the Christian life – after a few decades – a bit disappointing, if I may say that reverently. Disappointing in the sense that I was not on a spiritual high often enough. Hand on heart, I was putting one foot in front of the other most of the time, and not really experiencing any overflow of the love of God. You could say I was 'coping ugly'. And that's important. In fact, there are times when it is the only thing to do, especially when grief and loss tumble into your life, and brick walls are the norm when one comes to pray or read Scripture. C. S. Lewis wrote that grief blinds us to God. Temporarily. But I seemed to have been in a bad mood with God for about thirty years. And the galling thing was, others I knew seemed to be full of joy and fruit and grace. My faith was thorns and thistles, and it was time to find a sunnier upland than the gloomy forest in which I was wandering in circles.

It was an Ignatian-style retreat under a marvellous Jesuit spiritual director in the north of England. As a Protestant, when my mother heard I was going on an eight-day retreat at a Jesuit House she proclaimed, 'I'll be on ma knees tae stop them making ye a Catholic.' Poor old thing. She lived through the terrible sectarian divides in Northern Ireland and that left its bitter legacy. I had been raised there but God had seen fit to move me all over the world, and I had gone walkabout in the body of Christ as a result. I've had life-changing encounters with Polish Catholic youth leaders, Russian Orthodox rogue priests, Romanian underground Orthodox poets, ultra-charismatic Chinese rural house church leaders, snake-handling African-American Pentecostals, to say nothing of high church Anglicans and low church Brethren preachers.

And more!

But as I say, God and his overflows seemed to happen to them rather than to me.

Anyway, to cut a long story sideways, on retreat you have to still yourself. That's common to all retreats of course, and it is the hardest thing in the world. Wait. I tell a lie. It's actually the most impossible thing in the world, and you need to bend every sinew to get quiet before God, and then ask God if he will enable it.

For the first day or so you are flying. Every leaf speaks volumes. The sunset barks wholeness. Birds on the branches literally lift their legs to point you to the glory of God. OK, not literally, but you fill notebooks with the bursts of spiritual static.

And then it all goes quiet.

Really quiet.

And you wonder, what have I done wrong? Does God not want to speak to me? That's it starting. The noise is cancelled a little, and you begin – as you meditate through passages of Scripture – to discern individual voices that you are in constant dialogue with. Not only that, but you start to see the impact they have on your spiritual experience. How they might be snatching it away, or distracting you, or robbing you of a more genuine encounter with God.

As I started to figure out individual voices, I decided to name them. It's inevitable. My spiritual director asked me to meditate on the temptations of Jesus in the Gospel of Luke (Luke 4:1–13) and I began to think about what these diabolical voices were really asking of him. The first one is, essentially, turn stones into bread. Be a useful messiah. Solve the hunger crisis. And really Jesus is in the desert to do what Israel never did, which is to learn in forty days what they failed to in forty years; how to live by the words of God and not by bread alone (Deuteronomy 8:3). Right? That's why he is the new Israel, and why he goes into the desert in the first place.

And I was underway. How could I be useful? How was I trying to turn stones into bread? What was it about me that was trying to make a difference? In stillness the suggestions come slowly and clearly, because in a desert situation there are fewer distractions and less noise. The voices began to separate themselves and at the same time I began to see how dangerous they were and what, in particular, they were doing. Ultimately, they were dangerous because they took me away from myself, and from God. They made me absent myself from the present, and an encounter with God was somehow subverted.

First, there was **Glory Voice**. Glory Voice beckoned me to another land. 'Let's dream of you being the next Billy Graham,' it said. I fantasised that I was a great preacher, speaking to thousands over a weekend in a mega-church in China or the USA. Well known, with an international ministry. Maybe even a Study Bible named after me. It was a role that was very easy to colour in. The problem was, to entertain that voice I was going off to another planet. I had to leave where I was to go there. I wanted to be a great preacher. That was my role. And that voice was insistent – this is how you turn stones into bread. It started from an interaction with the Bible. It took the text, but led me off to planet dreamland. Someone might say, 'Yes, but isn't it great to have that kind of ambition for God?' And in my family of origin, the only type of people to be revered were great missionaries, preachers or evangelists. Focusing on riches was for stupid people. Getting into power positions was for sad losers. So it was no surprise that my dream role was a world-changing combination of missionary-preacher-evangelist. Maybe the retreat would come up with some key to unlock this famous destiny? But I was no longer listening to the text. I was absent. I was no longer able to have an experience of God, because I had put myself out of the arena of encounter.

Second, there was **Preaching Voice**. Not the same as Glory Voice, because I noticed that as I read the Scripture, I was preaching it out. Pages were filled with sermon outlines. What went wrong in the desert? Three points. The dreadful danger of manna. Five points. Three points on the power of Scripture to confound the devil. All with powerful illustrations. Walking around the room imagining I was speaking to thousands. 'Dear friends, I was retreating with the Lord on this passage and this word came to me. Let's think about why we need a desert, a thirst and a failure, in order to know the Lord.' Great stuff. But the problem was, the word was getting deflected out. I was reading the Scripture, having a great time, but turning the text into sermon sausages. I was getting great material, but the word was getting deflected. I was too busy proclaiming truth instead of discovering it. Again, I was no longer having an experience of God.

Third voice was **Sceptical Voice**. This voice was out to second guess any conclusion that I made. 'Oh you think you've got an understanding of that Scripture for yourself? Listen, you've probably just put your own experience in there, and read yourself into the passage.' Or if I felt something from God in the meditation, this voice would dart in and say, 'Hmm, this whole thing has just been a psychosomatic enterprise. God isn't speaking at all, or if he is, you can't be sure.' This voice started to introduce doubt that the whole enterprise of retreating was valuable at all. It's a big voice this, as we do live in a sceptical age and, often, the more educated you are, the stronger Sceptical Voice is. Again, the damage to experiencing God was clear – you discount what you have just enjoyed.

Another passage I was asked to meditate on was Acts 2. It was interesting how akin to Sceptical Voice was one of the reactions to Pentecost. One voice said, 'What can this mean?' (Acts 2:12). That's an adventurous voice. Those people realise something has happened they can't understand. They want to know more. They will receive an experience. But there is another voice, Sceptical Voice: 'They're just drunk, that's all' (Acts 2:13). They miss the birth of the church because they refuse to accept the phenomenon as it stands. They reduce it to a category that makes no demands on them. It's that 'nothing but-ery' that we find so much today. Prayer. It seems when we pray it lights up a distinct path in the brain. Yes, well, that just proves it's *nothing but* the firing of neurons. In an age full of mind-boggling science but pygmy philosophy, we are always finding the most intelligent people discounting spiritual activities on the assumption that if you have explained it physically or psychologically then that is utterly exhaustive of its reality. Open your newspaper and see the *nothing but-ery* process at work. But the point is, maybe these two voices are heard within us when something significant happens, and which one we listen to will determine whether we have an experience or not.

So the more I noticed these voices, the more I saw what they were trying to do, which was *to take me away from the present, and from myself.* You are deflected, or absented, or distracted, but the voices mean you no longer stay with God, attentively, in the present moment. I saw their danger. They all, in a different way, were preventing me from having an experience with God. No wonder life with God was dull. I wasn't showing up in the place of encounter. And that seemed quite diabolical in its effect.

To his credit, my spiritual director did not think I had taken leave of my senses. 'These voices are very important,' he said. 'You have seen that they are leading you away from Christ, not towards him.' But he also discerned that a huge change had taken place. He said, 'At first, it was the voices speaking through you. It wasn't you. You were identifying with the voices. Now, you are saying, "They are not me."' The preacher's voice was preventing Christ coming to me in any other form. The invitation was to define who I was now, so that the voices would no longer define me.

So it was no surprise that my spiritual director bade me take this notion again to the three temptations of Christ in the desert after the baptism. Jesus has just had his identity given to him in a voice from heaven: 'You are my dearly loved Son, and you bring me great joy.' But now that he knows who he is, what does he do? Jesus knows his worth; now he is led to find out his work. His identity is secure, but what kind of messiah should he be? And the devil will surely target that identity security.

So as I read the temptations, it seemed that the devil was out to give Jesus three false identities, and as Jesus rejected them, his own path became clearer. These voices – despite their diabolical origin – actually played a part in enabling him to know what kind of messiah to be.

Well, the devil starts off pretending to be a friend. It's like he says, 'OK, you're going to be a messiah? All right. Let me be your strategic advisor here on how to go about it.' First off, he gives him a *false priority*. 'You are going to become the most sought-after person in Israel because you are going to solve the hunger problem. Turning stones into bread will really be very useful in a way most religious types are not, and when you die, everyone will be so grateful.' I guess you could call it 'Useful Voice'.

But the whole point of these temptations of course is for the Gospel writer to show how Jesus is the true Israel, and that means he wins in the desert whereas Israel lost. Israel was not sent into the desert to learn how to eat manna. Manna was not the point of the experience. They were there to learn how to be a community that lived by the word of God, and only then could they model and proclaim the message of God. Jesus succeeds where Israel failed. It's the opposite of the diabolical suggestion – it's about proclaiming the message, not about the provision of bread. Throughout Jesus' ministry you can see that priority in action. Even when he encounters thousands of people who are weary and hungry, he teaches them first before feeding them (Mark 6:34). Words are more important than bread. Jesus learned the lesson.

If Jesus had not proclaimed a message, he would never have been a messiah. It is not that the provision of bread is unimportant. God did give the Israelites manna. But it is not *as* important. It is not what defines his identity and work. You could say, in a strange way, the voice helped. If it comes from the devil, and you reverse it, might you learn the true way?

Then the devil tries to give him *false power*. 'OK, you want to speak a message. All right, I'll work in with that. Now, the best way to get a hearing is to be a king. People listen to kings. They have to. You can chop their heads off if they don't. They are the people in the world whose words matter the most. Everyone has to listen to a king.' So he shows him all the kingdoms of the world. 'Here you are. Be king of them all. Only one condition . . . realise it's my gift!'

Again, this was why Israel was sent into the desert, to learn not to rely on strength, or skill, but God himself. They would conquer by being a community of faith. That's why Jericho fell but Ai did not. But they failed. Jesus said to the devil, 'That's not my path. I'll try the opposite way. I will see it as an advantage *not* to have all the connections of wealth and position, for how then would I know it was God doing the work? I will show the glory of God by starting out as a carpenter, not a king, a mendicant rabbi from a lowly town, not a high priest from the capital city.'

Finally the devil offers a *false security*. He essentially says, 'Right, if you want to do it that way, then you will have to really know God is with you. Better make sure you have heard correctly. In fact, you need to reassure yourself that God still loves you.' So he proposes this big spectacular deliverance scenario from the top of the temple. 'Make sure God really loves you. You can only know if you get these constant deliverances of spectacular power.'

So Jesus said, 'Actually, I don't need any such reassurance.' He remembered what God had said to him at the baptism. Nothing has changed. The heavens opened, the Spirit descended, and the voice of the Father spoke, 'You are my dearly loved Son, and you bring me great joy.' I don't need any signs. I don't need to keep pleading with God, 'Are you really on my side?' He told me who I am. Now, thanks to you, I know what I should do.

Israel never got to this point in the desert. They were always grumbling, always needing another sign that God was with them. And ironically, all that pleading took their energy away from seeing him. Every morning they had a miraculous provision of bread. Every evening they saw a pillar of fire. They had seen the waters of the Red Sea wipe out their enemies' armies. They saw water gush from flinty rock. They saw thick Jericho walls shatter into dust at the sound of trumpets. No generation was more surrounded by miracles. And yet. And yet, it didn't work. It was as if the signs dazzled rather than defined them. Jesus was to find the same in Israel. John's Gospel starts with seven great sign miracles, culminating in the raising of Lazarus. Does it help them to see Jesus? Not at all. They just get addicted to signs, rather than notice who the signs are pointing to.

But Jesus found his way.

Thanks to the devil, in a real sense.

This was all very well, and very worthy, but what about my experience of God? I was craving him, craving his presence, his grace, his love. Mere enlightenment would not do. More sermons to preach would not do. Could what happened to Jesus in the desert be a way the voices might assist me to find my way, a more intimate way? I wanted to know who I was and what I was to do. Could the voices actually help, or was my role just to shut them up in the name of Jesus? After all, if Jesus found the voice of Satan useful, could I find the voices useful, even if they might not be from so diabolical an origin?

So I went back to those three voices and sought to see if I could use them the same way. Glory Voice: this was the invitation to dream of being a Christian of great fame and power. So what was the opposite of that? A Christian who lives in obscurity and does not seek the limelight. Glory Voice was all about power. I wanted it. I wanted others to see I had it. But what if the way of glory was different as a result of Christ's ministry? The second part of John's Gospel is often called the Book of Glory, since it shows how Jesus is explicitly glorified. But the glory bit consists of a secret seminar, a mockery of a trial, a dreadful humiliating death, and a resurrection that climaxed in – wait for it – cooking breakfast for a few fishermen by the seashore in Galilee. That's a very different understanding of glory – not striving to do the big public stuff, but making room for God to do his will differently.

I know it doesn't seem like much as I put it into print. But at the time it lifted a burden. I didn't have to go and achieve for God. God wasn't measuring my success in terms of the size of the church or the fame of my words. I could stop striving and start trusting, and be content to know that a more powerful way might involve obscurity and suffering. It enabled me to give up some dreams that were in the way, in order to make room for the life that was waiting for me.

Oddly, a few months later I was reporting on the campaign of a famous healer-evangelist in Asia. Literally thousands were packing a small stadium and there was much whooping and yelling as so-and-so was healed of this-and-that. I was moving behind the scenes and talking to the producer who was televising this vast event. I noticed that there were some very interesting activities going on in other parts of the stage, but they were focusing the cameras only on the evangelist himself. So I said, 'Why don't you put your spotlight on the other parts of the stage? You are missing some great action.' He looked at me pityingly, and said, 'We're not allowed. If the Lord himself appeared on the stage the spotlight would still have to stay on the Rev _____ _____!' But what was really transformative for me was that for the first time I felt absolutely no envy or jealousy of this evangelist. Indeed, after an interview with him, I felt sorry for him. He had chosen the wrong sort of glory, and I could see the same anxiety and fear that had formerly characterised me, even as he settled back on deep leather seats in his private jet. His Glory Voice was winning. In fact, he knew himself so little he had fused with it. Mine had less grip, and God had more scope.

What about Preaching Voice? Preaching Voice was filled with the excitement of turning every Scripture into a powerful sermon or story. But what would be the opposite? How about this: Preaching voice says that the most important thing about the text is to learn it and proclaim it. Instead of me reading the Scripture, how about if the *Scripture reads me* and I simply enjoy it? And the agenda of having to know everything about that text, and agonise over how to convey it with great power and poise, would fall away. It's not that it is unimportant to think about how to understand and communicate, but the point is to communicate from a basis of an experience of love rather than an understanding of the mind. I had great material, but I was cold in heart. Could I read the Scripture in such a way that I felt God's love, and didn't get distracted into teaching mode, but sat in listening mode?

Again, that did not feel like much at the time. But it was fascinating that a few months later I happened to be living in Hong Kong and realised I was a half hour's walk from a Trappist monastery. And living in this Trappist monastery was one of the world's renowned teachers of what was called *contemplative prayer*, a monk called Basil Pennington, from New Jersey. I went along and began to learn how to sit in the presence of God, and not worry that I didn't have a sermon at the end of it. The focus was on *sitting with* God, not *speaking for* God. I could slow down, and know on a deeper level. And strangest of all, after that I happened to move cities and join a large church that unexpectedly threw open its preaching doors to me, and an old preaching dream came true in a new way.

And finally, what about Sceptical Voice? This was the voice that denigrated any experience of God. It offered a naturalistic explanation as definitive. And it was deeply internalised in me because I was educated in the social sciences in an atmosphere where religion was regarded as an epiphenomenon, something that was caused by something else. So I thought, well, what is the opposite of that? The opposite might be that no single explanation of any experience of God exists, but that three or more could be equally valid. Maybe it's crude to reduce spiritual experience to the material. Sounds a bit like a scientific formula, I admit. But the intention of Sceptical Voice is to create a crisis of confidence. Whatever you say you have experienced of God, it is not allowed to attain the status of truth: 'You can't say that! You can't know that! You are probably wrong! The physicists know more about this, and you know nothing. Let the biologists sort that out – you don't belong.'

But this was a lie. This needed to be talked back to, and I happened upon Richard Dawkins' virulent broadside against religion in the wake of 9/11. The book was so extreme, so angry, and so religious sounding, I realised with a rush of insight: *this man lives by faith!* He just put his faith in random collisions of chance and necessity, but he needed more faith in that random process to bring us this beautiful world than I needed to affirm the existence of God. His book was more religious than the Bible. Suddenly, the absurdity of assuming that a physical description of the universe was in any sense exhaustive of it was exposed for what it was – a desperate faith position.

Also, what was clear was that his argument could not touch me, because he was telling me that religion cannot work. But I had seen it work in the lives of my parents. It was good for them. It made them good people, careful parents who loved their neighbours and were model citizens. They provided the social capital that made a society a pleasant place to live in. But he was saying nothing good could come from religion. So it was simple for me – don't walk away from something that works, even if you don't understand it.

The problem was, so much of my life, my faith, my inter-action with God, was not making any sense, but I could not relax into this mystery. I felt oppressed by it, as if failing to explain it meant it could not be true. And when I came to speak of religious experience, I felt I had none. But this was a lie, and indeed one of the primary gifts of expert spiritual direction is the valuing of your own spiritual experience. The voice of disparagement was put in its place, and I could enjoy what could no longer be explained but merely enjoyed, or intimated, or glimpsed. What was never sufficient before suddenly became a prime bulwark of experience. I could grow up. I could believe that my own experience of God was true, but true in a way that built on scientific truth and went beyond it to a deeper embrace of what truth really was – the kind of truth you don't just assent to but live by!

I suppose there is in us a mad belief that we have to understand or we cannot believe. Maybe that was what was bothering Job. But as I once heard at a funeral, 'Because we are human, we want to know why, yet because we are human, we cannot know why.' Job learned to be content not to understand the mysteries of the universe, but to relax into his status as a creature. He was assuming he could understand it all. But only the Creator can, and that's what's wrong with the world. The failure to accept that we are creatures and not the Creator is the source of all unhappiness, and reversing that is the royal road to joy. Hey, that'll preach – or is that Preaching Voice roaring back?

Sceptical Voice has its value, but it needs to learn its place. The processes of doubt are what keep us honest. Questioning orthodoxy is the way to learn more. We are not meant to be naive or credulous. Remember at the end of the book of Job God speaks to the man with the questions, not to the people with the answers. I had a route. I had a lifeline. I had hope. I could stand.

And I could stand and walk because these voices that were oppressing me, and trying to take me away from the arena of experience with God, actually lost their power and gave me light, once I had reversed their advice, like Jesus in the desert. Voices can set you free . . . if you know how to talk back to them.

I'm not saying just reverse the advice of the voice and you'll find your path to glory. Some voices, as we will see, are almost wholly true, and to reverse them would be a tragedy. But the experience showed me how to begin. It warned me of their power. It revealed their essence – to snatch me away from an experience of God himself.

And more. Now that I could have an experience of God, this pleasant insight could be accessed – perhaps these voices never leave us for the very good reason that they can be useful . . . if we know how to deal with them!

4

How Voices Mess Us Up

ENOUGH OF ME. How about others? How about you?

Let me keep on reinforcing the idea about the sheer importance of the voices, since – understandably – it takes so long just to get used to the idea of them and not feel weird or schizoid to even be talking about one's inner discourse.

Here are the stories of four people. They are true stories, though disguised to maintain their privacy. In no particular order, they are:

- Defective Deborah
- Get-Ahead Gerald
- Successful Sally
- Never-Good-Enough Nigel

Defective Deborah

If Deborah sent an email to someone, and they failed to reply in an hour, she was worried. If they didn't in a day, she was frantic. She would pore over the email, wondering how she could have given offence. She took great care over all emails, even drafting them longhand sometimes in order to get the tone right. In two days she would be drafting an apology that she had put her thoughts badly.

She thought the world was cross with her. It was her fault that it was. Somehow she had screwed up.

She had a voice so powerful it dominated all her interactions with the world: *'Deborah, you are defective!'*

This voice had a source. It was probably her mother, who was very hard on her. The mother had had her own share of pain, and to shield Deborah from the disappointments she had experienced, she made it a priority to tell Deborah that she really kept messing up all the time, so that Deborah would not try to be happy. And that would make her happy . . . in a realistic, as-much-as-you-can-expect kind of way. Weird? Welcome to the world.

But Deborah knew none of this.

She meets an old friend for coffee in town. Two days later the friend has not replied or sent a cheery that-was-fun note, though Deborah in the meantime has tweeted three. She starts to replay the conversation they had. Was it the tone? She would rehearse the way she had said something. Or scour the conversation for errors. Or worry that something was going on in the life of her friend that she did not know about. Wait, it was worse than that, she concluded. The friend had kept it from her. Maybe the friend no longer trusted her. That would send her into more internal scouring of her words and actions that must have meant she was no longer worthy of her friend's confidences.

Defective Deborah was miserable, and frankly, most of the time, the anxiety she maintained was completely unjustified. Those who failed to get back quickly by email were just busy. Or they forgot. That friend who didn't tweet any thanks was having trouble with her Twitter account. Or whatever. Deborah was actually very beloved of a lot of people, but she could never relax into that love, never take it for granted, and never really enjoy it, because – soon – she was going to screw up.

Never mind that Deborah is a person who has risen high in the world. She has a doctorate from a top university, gained tenure before she was forty, and regularly lectures around the world on a subject on which she is commonly acknowledged to be an expert. Her anxiety and second guessing make her a great researcher, because she checks everything, is very thorough, and always gets back to everyone, even late at night or on holiday. She doesn't think she's much. She's waiting for the day – like a lot of academics actually – she discovers she's really a fraud and knows nothing at all.

That's a voice. See how it robs her of her joy, her peace, her satisfaction in great attainment. It's so profound it is difficult for her to talk to God. The Big Guy sees how defective she really is. She can't hide who she is from him. She fears him, and is reluctant to talk to him, and yet at the same time she is anxious to overcome her defects and tries very hard to be good in his sight.

She's weary from the worry of it all though.

One voice, and it's ruining her.

Get-Ahead Gerald

Get-Ahead Gerald probably knows Defective Deborah, but he would never guess at her anxieties. He's not interested. He's at the top of the tree, and boy he deserves to be. He didn't have a great start in life. He remembers getting dragged by the hand by his mother around the streets of Glasgow every Friday. She was aiming to intercept her husband (Gerald's father) with his pay packet before he got to the pub. Otherwise the week's wages would be lost to drink by the hopeless drunk his dad was. Gerald rose out of that by telling himself he was the best, was going to be the best, and deserved the best.

He studied hard, picking law because even at eighteen years old he had the wit to see it was a lucrative profession. But not for him the Jaguar-owning lifestyle of the local solicitor, filing dull deeds of marriage, divorce settlements and house purchases. He headed off to the Far East with a multinational. No one worked harder. No one played harder. It was a tough world but he had boundless confidence from a voice that pushed him on: 'I'm the best at mergers and acquisitions.'

Maybe he was, or maybe he wasn't. But he landed in Hong Kong at just the right time to get a ringside seat for a period of merger mania. His pay was colossal. So were the perks. Free housing. Use of a yacht every weekend. Regular flights in the company jet. Suites in hotels overlooking the world's cleanest, sparkling oceans in resorts in the Bahamas, Belize, and Bali – and those are only the places beginning with B.

The downside was that he didn't have time for much else. Or anyone else. That included four wives, who loved him but left in despair when he just couldn't fit them into his professional schedule. There were three kids; he knew that much because he funded them through university. But they never came to visit. Oh wait, two of them had but Gerald needed to fly to Switzerland and cancelled on them.

Gerald's voice was positive, not negative: *I am the best at mergers and acquisitions!* But it was a voice that confined him to shining entirely through his profession, and he didn't have much left over for the other joys of life. This came to him one day at the long bar of a ritzy restaurant in New York. One moment he was advising the CEO on how to tie up an agreement with Chinese counterparts, the next he heard beeping sounds and it gradually dawned on him he was in ICU.

The CEO came to visit. Flowers. Grapes. A pat on the shoulder, and a line that nearly gave Gerald a second heart attack on the spot: 'Take your time, Gerald; your deputy tied the agreement up so well we can spare you here for a few weeks.' The CEO thought he was helping, but Gerald suddenly got a burst of insight. 'At sixty-three I knew nothing about the fundamental questions of life. I knew everything about the law in mergers and acquisitions, and yet I was really quite dispensable. How was I going to fill my life now that I could no longer travel and work the long hours required to shine at my job?'

So Get-Ahead Gerald turned into Get-Serious Gerald. At sixty-three. It's never too late, but look at the power of that voice of achievement, which kept him rich, busy, and even scornful of the act of asking the deeper questions of life. The voice took him away from himself, and he never knew it, until he nearly died.

Successful Sally

She was the go-to person for management issues in several administrations in the US capital. No one knew better than Sally how to cut through red-tape and make a reform happen. She oozed confidence, and marriage to a high-profile donor to the party did not do her status as a key mover and shaker any harm at all. She was given gongs and awards and she had a big house in an area of Washington DC that said to any driver, 'We've made it and you haven't.' She could afford to eat at all the right restaurants, and enjoyed the nodding and bobbing game with the city's in-group. What could be better than to be enjoying steak at the Palm on 19th Street while a Secretary of State raised a salaam, a CNN anchor-man greeted her by name, and a roomful of interns looked past their dates and coveted the status she enjoyed?

But the perks of status were actually of little interest to her. She was driven by a civic-minded father, who drummed into her the idea that public service was the only way to build a better society. 'The private sector is only out for profit,' he would tell her when she was in her teens. 'It's public administration that looks out for everyone.' If he had been living in Britain he would have been called a Socialist: 'The market doesn't distribute fairly – it can't'! he told her; but in the USA he was simply a Democrat.

A voice drove her – *serve the people, not the company.* However, the problem was that her party lost an election, and she had to go out into the private sector. They were glad to have her, and her salary tripled, but her satisfaction dived. That voice – which had validated her through all the political infighting of a US administration – now mocked her with a devastating force: *you're just making money for yourself – you're just propping up the shareholders – you've stopped caring about your society.*

It didn't matter that the voice was lying – in this new job she was probably doing more social good than in all the time she had spent in government. Her work did not fit her father's template about what living a good life was all about. After years of success, she succumbed to a nervous breakdown. She couldn't handle the voice . . . and the more she succeeded in the private sector, the more she felt she was wasting her life!

Successful Sally did manage a turnaround. She was able to turn down the volume of her father's voice, and turn up the knob on a newer one – 'I am enjoying this work because it is good work.' She ended up as a still-life painter. Her life's work was to urge people to slow down and see, and she loved nothing more than to take a group of strangers through the still-life masters' collection of the National Gallery in DC.

She knows how to see a skull, a walnut and a peeled lemon.

But it cost her a breakdown. And a change-of-life orientation.

Never-Good-Enough Nigel

Nigel was a preacher. A good one, though he wanted to be the greatest. He wouldn't admit it but his library was the best in the land for homiletics books, and every sermon his heroes had preached – Chrysostom, Luther, Bushnell, Brooks, Morgan and Lloyd-Jones – he had rehearsed in front of a mirror. It worked, after a fashion. By forty he had a huge church with thousands who hung on his every word each weekend. Publishers feted him to turn his sermon series into gold. He allowed it, though his ghost writer did the heavy lifting. His diary was full for years to come, and it was nearing time to establish a foundation in his name to put his sermon corpus onto radio shows and the internet for future generations.

God had blessed him. God had prospered him. God had made a way.

Except that this wasn't good enough.

Nigel was a great preacher, but most people in the land did not know his name. He was no Billy Graham. Nigel urged his church to do social work, but he was no Martin Luther King Jnr. Nigel was a tolerable scholar, but he was no Raymond E. Brown. Nigel was a good entertainer, but he was no Rodney Howard-Browne. Nigel preached through the book of Acts ten times, but revival never followed his ministry. He was no Charles Finney.

This galled him. Because he wasn't good enough.

Not good enough to be a world-changer.

He knew this was irrational, and he was irritated to feel so disappointed that he was not a world-renowned amalgam of the evangelistic fame of Billy Graham, the social power of

Martin Luther King Jnr, and the revival-bringing power of Charles Finney. But he couldn't help it.

Only his wife knew that Nigel was a functioning alcoholic. Because every time he preached and revival didn't follow, he was crushed. He never admitted this publicly, and his wife only guessed. But his drinking was starting to get out of control. He just could not handle the disappointment.

It drove him into the limelight like never before. If he went to that conference, and this convention, and heard the roar of thousands of people laughing at a joke he had been telling since he was sixteen, he could tell himself that he still had it, and was destined to change the world.

But back in his hotel room, after a few despairing prayers – because revival had not followed his talk – it was time for the minibar, and a pleasant oblivion to block out the horrible voice growing larger with every member added to his church: *You are not anointed enough to be my instrument to save the world!*

Nasty voice that. Not anointed enough? There was nothing Nigel could do. Yes, he could train, beseech, fast, organise everything just so, but the terror of knowing that if God didn't really want to show up it wouldn't happen, was becoming impossible to bear. After twenty-five years in ministry, he was becoming conscious that his great breakthrough should have happened by now. It hadn't come, and the voice kept whispering – 'You've not got the anointing . . . you're kinda crap for Jesus, aren't you?'

Nigel wasn't good enough to deserve the anointing.

What a nasty, crazy, lying voice.

But it was turning him into a mid-life alcoholic.

And that's where Nigel is today. You may well have heard a sermon from him, or his type. He's got great hair, a resonant voice, a shimmering suit, fantastic material, and he oozes victory. But he's up there because he wants to be God's blessed servant. He wants to be Moses, David, Peter and Paul all in one. And it galls him that it would appear he is none of them. And he will soon blame God rather than himself.

That realisation will bring him down.

Or his addictions will come into the open. And they will bring him down.

And few will care.

Voices. They can really screw you up!

Just four people. Quite possibly they keep their inner discourse to themselves. Their spouses may only get a hint. And remember that two of those voices were positive, not negative. For Successful Sally and Get-Ahead Gerald the voices were not tearing them down, just tearing them up, because they were taking them away from their true selves.

Positive and negative voices work differently to do exactly the same thing, which is to take us away from our true selves. Positive voices are voices of achievement or ambition, and they seek to distract us and shrink our identity down to what we do externally. Negative voices are voices of inadequacy, and they seek to disempower us, and shrink our identity down internally, so that we are less than what we should be. Negative voices weaken our internal self-esteem, whereas positive voices try to tie the self to what lies outside it.

The four people you have just read about are not famous. But the business of managing voices is central to success, real success. Samuel Beckett, the great Irish playwright who like so many Irish men of letters preferred to live anywhere but Ireland, struck a new line in literature, especially in his play *Waiting for Godot*, making waiting for God – and waiting for nothing – as entertaining as it was pointless. Not for him the arc of transformation in each character, or plots of antagonist versus protagonist, or hero journeys from impossible odds to dragon-slaying. No, just a clever, bleak humour to distract us from the void, yet at the same time make us face the void (yes he was clever).

He got the Nobel Prize for Literature for his achievements. And is, apparently, the fourth most biographed figure in history (after Jesus, Mohammed and Napoleon).

But he only achieved as an artist because he figured out how to manage his voices. Critic Robert Douglas-Fairhurst suggests that Beckett's early stuff was sub-Joycean posing. But this changed because,

> Only when he came to write his plays did Beckett discover how to manage the voices in his head, like the solitary child Hamm describes in *Endgame*, 'who turns himself into children, two, three, so as to be together, and whisper together, in the dark'. The theatre tethered these voices to real bodies and gave them stories to share.[1]

---

[1] Quote from 'The Collected Poems of Samuel Beckett ed by Sean Lawlor and John Pilling: review' by Robert Douglas-Fairhurst, *Telegraph* (2012), http://www.telegraph.co.uk/culture/books/bookreviews/9447340/ The-Collected-Poems-of-Samuel-Beckett-ed-by-Sean-Lawlor-and-John-Pilling-review.html.

Beckett found his literary metier because he discovered *how to manage the voices in his head*.

Are you an artist? Maybe you are on the verge of greatness, but are getting nowhere? Maybe the one thing required is to know how to manage the voices in your head.

Just a thought.

On a more negative-positive note, consider the case of poor John Galliano, the Brit genius designer of the House of Dior until he was filmed by a mobile phone hurling anti-Semitic abuse in a Paris bar in 2011. Few thought he would ever make it back after his sacking, and he was in a bad way. In a rare interview he put it down to his voices: 'I just needed to learn how to stop the voices in my head,' he said.

The voice was a pretty mad one it seemed. It deprived him of all sense of proportion. He thought designing was all that mattered in life, so you could say it was a classic achievement voice. 'Before,' he admitted, 'work was the most important thing in my life, not my health, which is insanity.' He would work obsessively through the night, not even realising it was five in the morning. 'The creative process is all-consuming, and that's something in me – one of my many character defects – that I have to keep in check.' In his pomp, one assistant would hold his cigarettes, the other his lighter. He couldn't even do ordinary tasks, because everything had been done for him.

He got it, though. He was cut off from reality. And that was bad.

It took a fit of drunkenness, and the sack, to wake him up to the realisation that he was 'away from himself', like the Prodigal Son, and dangerously out of touch with reality. His first act was to get into rehab and contact Shaolin monks, who taught him to meditate. This saved him. Meditation gave him the ability to detach from his driving voices of achievement. He's back in employment. Dior's doors are forever closed, but he is head designer with Maison Margiela.

One of the world's most creative clothing designers got his life back . . . because he learned to deal with his voices.[1]

But managing one's voices is not just a matter of getting a couple of creatives back on track. Dealing with them can determine how much civic strife and danger we all have to face in everyday life. We live in days of terror from extremists. Our greatest fear is that they might radicalise themselves on the internet. I suppose the good news is that they don't. No one radicalises themselves. It takes others. It takes a group.

But that is the nub of the worry. Because when you join a group, you adopt an uncritical view of the world, and you stop letting other voices in that might save you from the violence the group insists upon committing.

A few years ago the BBC aired a brilliant drama written by Guy Hibbert, *Five Minutes of Heaven*. It starred Liam Neeson and James Nesbitt, with Neeson playing a Protestant terrorist who had shot a Catholic in the Troubles. The killing had been witnessed by the victim's brother, who was blamed by his mother for not saving his brother, which was understandable if totally irrational, but he had been carrying that guilt for thirty-three years. Neeson's character served twelve

---

[1] Quotes from 'The fall and rise of John Galliano' by Claudia Croft, *The Sunday Times*, 5 June 2016.

years before getting out and beginning reconciliation work. He explains his journey before the proposed meeting with the victim's brother in terms of voices. There were the voices of his group, and they were all he listened to. Those voices told him that to harm a Catholic would bring him respect and, sure enough, when he shot him he was applauded into the pub. But what he saw later was that he did it because 'there were no voices on my side. None on my side of the town. Not on my estate. No one was telling me anything other than that killing is right. It was only in prison when I heard that other voice.' And so Muslim extremists are causing terror today because, in the same way, they never get to hear any voices telling them there is a better way.

The film made a big impact on me because I spent my teenage years growing up in Belfast, and had also felt the pull of sectarianism. This character was authentic, and the only difference between myself and that person was not the degree of bigoted indignation: I had it too. It was the air you breathed. The difference was, I was exposed to other voices, like, 'You can't build anything up with a gun,' and, 'Catholics are also loved by God and we have to get along,' that prevented me from being gobbled up into the group and walled off from an alternative way of seeing and defining myself. Because I heard a few more voices, and paid attention to them, I narrowly avoided becoming a terrorist.

All this to say . . . voices – they mess you up!

Or they can save you.

Got it?

You've got at least one.

Or two.

Or three.

And the chances are, they are ruining your life in inverse proportion to how much you are aware of them.

Don't feel weird. Feel normal.

Let's go to war with them.

And win!

Here's how.

5

How to Identify Your Voices

Up front, let me warn you. There are two sets of initials you are going to get very fed up with before long: SNN and ADD. The first refers to *Still, Notice and Name*, and is the process we simply cannot skip in identifying what our various voices may be. The second refers to *Absent, Dismiss, Deflect*, and tells us what our various voices are doing to take us away from our deeper identity.

Still, notice and name is crucial because a voice's power depends significantly on its speed. It suggests something so fast that all we register it as is an emotional charge. 'I'm no good' doesn't come to us as a sentence, but a rush of despair. 'I'd rather be someone else' comes to us as a soft desire to float away, disconnect and dream. 'I'll get even' presents as a cold anger. A voice is a fast mugger. Its skill is to overwhelm us so quickly that it takes the reins without us appearing to surrender them.

A voice wants to be our auto-pilot.

So if speed is its tactic, stillness is what unmasks it. It's like slowing down a film so that we see the action frame by frame.

This is where we hear a voice distinctly – as opposed to the party babble of the heart – and sense its power.

But becoming still is one of the world's hardest activities. I remember, on a Christian ashram in India, learning how to pray. It was a week-long activity, but for six of the seven days all we did was sit in a posture that did not cause cramp, and learn to control our breath. 'When are we going to get onto prayer?' I asked, a little frustrated. The reply was, 'Prayer is a conversation with God, but we are incapable of holding it until we can still our bodies, because only then will we hear the whisper of God's voice.'

There's a line from John Donne that goes, 'My body licenceth my soule,' which I understand to mean that you can only fellowship with God as much as your body lets you. Thomas Aquinas wrote, 'There is nothing in our minds which was not first in our senses.' Like it or not, our bodies seem to have been designed by God to form an aperture for the spirit; close it up and there is little we can receive; open it wide and the possibilities are glorious. Holiness is a physical business.

I did not come from a tradition that involved the body in holiness. Throw yourself into prayer and Bible study, said the preachers, and holiness will be the automatic result. To be fair, I did see some people for whom this worked, but they were few, and all of them were preachers who had to get into the Scriptures not out of love but out of necessity. It took me many years to admit it had never worked for me.

Stillness is a massive industry now. The mindfulness craze in the West shows no sign of abating – the Headspace app is one of the most popular; mindfulness courses are offered even on the NHS, and are not just another wellbeing accessory for the wealth-health-and-capped-teeth brigade. But mindfulness – although prospering in a secular form – has come from religion, and it is there that a more rounded understanding is presented that shows that stillness in itself can carry at least half the healing of troubled voices. Perhaps the clearest exponent of this is Fr Thomas Keating. Borrowing from Thomas Merton and his idea of the 'false self', Keating maintains that our ego has trained us to cope with life through manufacturing three programmes for happiness which turn into programmes for misery. They are our desire for affection and esteem, for security and survival, and for power and control. Especially between the ages of four and eight they become socialised into us from all sides – from television, family, society. They become energy centres that begin to define our personality. You can go into the priest-hood, for example, out of a desire for power and control, and you may get it, but it will not make you happy, because you have over-identified with the programme at the expense of your deeper identity, your true self. A true self is not in the grip of these childhood programmes, but is centred in God, and the grasping anxiety of the ego falls away. I'll explain more about this later, but the point here is to notice Keating's solution: silence. Or, in his terms, contemplative prayer.

Twenty minutes morning and evening of contemplative prayer, which is the conscious placing of oneself into a still state before God, including the stilling of the whirring of thoughts, will provide a 'divine paid-for vacation from the clamour of the false self', Keating claims. It's all in the pause. If you can train your body not to respond to the voice, auto-matic force is disrupted and a choice point is created. Of course, you have to make this choice, and that's where the five strategies for dealing with our voices come in. We are going to make much of these five ways in subsequent chapters, but stillness is the start of it all, the beginning of refusing to grant space to our controlling voices.

Well, stillness itself may not seem like much, but it is surprisingly transformative. One of my heroes is the great economist E. F. Schumacher, who gave us the seminal *Small is Beautiful* in 1973, the subtitle of which says it all: *A study of economics as if people mattered*! Schumacher came to his views as a result of a very simple technique, by devoting fifteen minutes a day to relaxation and concentration exercises. Just 1 per cent of the 24 hours, he said – what did he have to lose (and trust an economist to work it out to a percentage)? The results staggered him:

> From then on everything began to change . . . the modest practice of allowing some degree of inner stillness to establish itself – if only for fifteen minutes a day, to start with – led to these unsuspected discoveries: like a Geiger counter, the inward parts started to react and in fact to *burn* as soon as my mind found itself in contact with the real thing – what shall I call it? – with 'Truth'.

Schumacher began to understand words and concepts at a depth he had previously not experienced, and gained such a conviction of the reality of human dignity that he began a hugely influential movement that saw humans as much more connected – and therefore much more responsible – for the environment in which we all have to co-exist.

All this is to say . . . stillness matters. So how do we get still so we can tune into the voices? A massive literature awaits, but start here if you like.

All you need is an egg timer and a chair.

Sit down on the chair. Back firm and your feet fully on the ground. Start the egg timer. Maybe try and get a fifteen-minute one, or even just set your phone timer.

Shut your eyes, and just let your mind roam over the parts of your body, starting at your feet and working up. Just notice what may be going on. A bit of tension. Flex a little. Let it go. Work your way up. Explore your lower back. Carrying any tension? Tense and release if it helps. All the way up to shoulders and face. Then notice the rhythm of your breathing. Just focus on the sensation of your breath at the tip of your nose.

See if you can go for fifteen minutes.

As for thoughts, let them go. Just sit. Don't think. If thoughts come (and they will) just place them gently onto an imaginary barge and let it float downriver. Be kind to them. Be kind to yourself. Don't get attached at this point. Let your anxieties slip into the background a little.

That's it. That's the hardest thing in the world.

Well, that and giving your life savings away.

Do that regularly. Even if it is just for five minutes at first. You don't have to become a monk and concoct a whole superstructure of silence and discipline. Just build up a taste for these moments of stillness. And don't give in to that voice that says, 'This is a waste of time . . . I should be thinking about important things.' Time for that later.

Now then, take that stillness, and try this exercise of noting and naming voices. We'll try some boxes to start with, and then some lists. Doesn't that sound interesting? OK, I'm desperately trying to hold you here.

Look at the four boxes below:

AS A CHILD		AS A YOUNG ADULT	
- family	- bullies	- family	- friends
- teachers	- church	- work	- church
- peers	- other	- media	- other

CURRENTLY		TODAY
- self	- church	What are you longing to hear from someone/ from somewhere?
- family	- friends	
- work	- other	
- media		

What message did you get about yourself? First box, AS A CHILD. Take a good ten minutes to think about what messages you were given about yourself from your family, your teachers, your peers, maybe a bully or two, even your church. Just write them down as they come. You may have come from a church culture that told you that you were a 'squashed crumb for Jesus'. You might have come from a family that said, 'You've got to be really great at music, or sport, because we are.'

Second box, AS A YOUNG ADULT. Again, run through the various possible origins – from yourself, your family, friends, work, media maybe, church, and so on. It is here that some very cruel voices can emerge, especially from peers.

I'm looking back over life from my fifties right now and let me tell you the subsequent decades after the teenage years are a breeze compared to the naked hostilities, bullying, insults, cat-calls and general character assassinations that take place in the average secondary school. What was your nickname? Who broke your heart? What did they say? Who mended your heart? What did they say? It's a tough phase of life. Has to be. You're trying to stop living life at second hand. Keep writing those messages down.

Third box: CURRENTLY. What messages do you get about yourself today? Again, go down the list of sources. How does your church define you? Do you like to think you are what Apple call you (if you buy their products) – a cool creative? What news source do you consume? How does it make you feel? I know someone who gets the *Financial Times* at the weekend, and she scours the property section, drooling over property she could never in ten lifetimes afford. 'It tells me, *you are poor and all you have is dreams*,' she admits. What about your church? Are they always bugging you for money? Does it make you wish you were richer? What are your workmates saying about you? You might even dare to Google yourself or YouTube yourself and discern what messages are being sent there.

Finally, there's a fourth box, TODAY. What message are you longing to hear from someone? Maybe it's 'I love you' from someone who has died. Maybe it's 'You really matter to me' from your child, who seems to treat you like a piece of furniture. What would you love God to say to you? Tune in to a deeper longing – that's where the better voices come from.

After all that, make a list of the messages in your four boxes. It may be a list like this:

I'm no good.
I'd rather be someone else.
I've missed my chance . . . I'll never make it.
I'm going to be the best.
I'll get even . . . I'll show them.
You are so unattractive.
I just want to disappear.
Just grin and bear it.
You should be enjoying God more.
Everything will sort itself out if you just stay busy.
I want to leave a legacy.
If only I had more money.
You had better make the world a better place.
I have to be useful.
Everyone's better than me, especially better-looking.
I have nothing special to offer.
It never helps to complain.
I always do my best and it's never good enough.

And so on. Whatever your list, start by distinguishing positive from negative voices with a plus or a minus. A negative voice is usually to do with inadequacy. It targets who you are, and tries to tell you that you're a loser. It seeks to disempower and shrink your identity down internally, until all you can see is your inadequacies. A positive voice is usually to do with achievement. It targets what you are doing, and tries to satisfy you with success.

But it's also a shrinkage – it's shrinking you down to what you do externally. Being and doing – the voices are nothing if not comprehensive in their attack, but it's often the positive voices that slip under the radar, because we tend to assume they are beneficial; but remember, we are talking about the fight to be who we really are. Success is brilliant at deflecting us from that.

Thomas Merton, the great modern monastic, knew the power of this. He once said, 'If I had a message to my contemporaries it is surely this: Be anything you like, be madmen, drunks, and bastards of every shape and form, but at all costs avoid one thing: success. If you are too obsessed with success, you will forget to live. If you have learned only how to be a success, your life has probably been wasted.' That's the power of positive voices.

OK, check and see if there are voices common to the first three boxes. This gives a clue to a voice's persistence and power. Divide them into two groups; voices that are still significant, mark with a 1, and those that are not so significant currently, don't rate, or give a 2.

Now we've got a list of your most significant voices. The next thing is to give them a name that describes how they make you feel. A name gives you a handle, and really helps for recognition. We need this because dealing with a voice is a speed game, and handles help.

'I'm no good.' Perhaps call that *Worthless Voice*.

'That can't be true.' Perhaps call that *Doubt Voice*.

'It's too difficult for me.' Perhaps call that *Frightened Voice*.

'I've missed my chance.' Perhaps call that *Resigned Voice*.

'I love doing this because it is going to make me famous.' Perhaps call that *Glory Voice.*

'I'm going to get to the top of this organisation.' Perhaps call that *Power Voice.*

'I've got to be rich.' Perhaps call that *Materialistic Voice.*

You get the idea. *Still, notice and name* – it's the first way to get a handle on what our voices are.

But the point of all this is to get a sense of what our voices are actually doing to us. Are they running and ruining our lives or not? Most of these voices you have identified are out to commit an act of theft – they want to steal your identity. They are out to prevent you living out of a greater self. They are out to stop you from praying that beautiful prayer of St Ignatius: 'May I never seek or choose to be other than you intend or wish.'

So how do most of these voices accomplish identity theft?

Welcome to the second rubric: ADD. The voices want to give us ADD syndrome. The essence of a voice is that it wants to take us away from the world of experiencing God. It wants to make sure we do not present our whole self before God. It offers a substitute for the real, divine thing. We are creatures who crave an interaction with God, but we have inside and outside us mechanisms keeping us away from this fearful yet glorious interaction. If you want it in Augustinian terms, he says to God in his famous *Confessions*, 'You were within me, but I was without.' So many voices are there to keep us 'without', and failing to meet God 'within'. Here are just three ways this can happen.

How to Identify Your Voices

1. Absent

A voice wants us to absent ourselves from the arena of experience. Some voices specialise in taking you away from yourself, so you are just not present. We fail to show up to the present moment, and in that way, we fail to show up to our life.

A good therapist is able to tell whether a person is present or not. Fantasy voices are classically good at this. I like to call this 'the Marilyn Monroe move'. If you are nobody, she said, you can't be somebody else unless you become somebody else. So a voice sets out to make you someone you are not. Dreams are a big clue. Or where we go when we put music on. Music is often a way of slipping into another dimension, and pretending we are someone else.

For some people, this voice is brazen. 'I want to be a Formula One driver.' Fine. But it's a fantasy voice if the person saying it is forty and doesn't have much experience of cars. The voice is offering a role to occupy in fantasy land. We float off. Yes, there we are, in a Ferrari, just edging out Schumacher and Senna in a dive for the chequered flag. Perhaps a soundtrack is taking us there.

But that person is absent from their life. They have opted for a parallel dimension, perhaps to avoid the disappointment of the real world. The voice says it's better to pretend to be somebody than to face being a nobody – at least according to certain criteria of fame, fortune or daring-do.

Sensual voices are similar. A voice like, 'I am a super handsome person who will slay the ladies/men.' Perhaps there is a lack of sexual experience or excitement, but this voice can drive a person to hopeless porn addiction, for example. They think they are having a great experience by pretending online to be this Brad Pitt or Angelina Jolie but, in actual fact, they have blown their pleasure circuits by overdosing on adrenalin, and they are not actually feeling anything anymore. They are going numb. They are absent. The voices are creating a new person, called 'No-self'. It can be very difficult to deal with people who have these voices because they are not 'in' when you are talking to them. The voice is trying to keep you in a false dimension so you can't really have an experience because you are not in the real world. A fantasy voice may be one of the defining voices of our age because we are surrounded by media trying to make us wish we are someone we are not, or somewhere we are not, or have things we have not, and our real world seems so dull and tawdry by comparison, it's better to just set off and be part of another imaginary world.

This is not to say that all entertainment that transports us is wrong. A good book or film should provide a character with whom we identify. But it's only healthy if you can come back to who you are, or to becoming a better you.

I see this in church all the time. The preacher gets up, and you learn to go onto a different mental planet rather than stay in the church listening to someone who is diabolically boring or dull. Withdrawal from reality has taken place, and a voice beckons you off somewhere else.

That kind of voice just doesn't let you turn up to your closest friends, to life, and ultimately, to God.

You end up not turning up to your own life.

2. Dismiss

Another type of voice accepts that we have had an experience, but it snatches that experience away by dismissing it. 'That didn't really happen.' 'I was not thinking straight at the time.' *If absent means you don't turn up to have an experience, dismiss means you refuse to rate or value the experience you have had.* Deny or dismiss. Remember those two voices that occur at Pentecost? One says, 'How can this be?' The other says, 'They're drunk – that's all.' That's dismiss. Those people saw it happen. Look at what they turn their back on. Tongues of fire. Languages of the world supernaturally spoken. Babel reversed. A world re-wired right. But they have dismissed it. They will walk away from it. They will never become Pentecost people.

Cynical voices are uppermost here. They deny validity to what happens. 'Yes, I may have spoken in tongues, but I was vulnerable and it's all psychosomatic anyhow.' Indeed, we have a whole world of *scientism* that is out to completely refute the valuing of any religious experience, at least in the West. Or a voice that belittles what has gone on – 'It wasn't that significant.' Academic voices are strong here, because they can paralyse us. I used to live in Cambridge and know well that many people have detached from life in order to look at it that they can no longer re-enter it. They can't experience anything.

3. Deflect

Yes, you are having an experience, and enjoying it, but the voice then deflects this experience so that it won't go deep enough for true transformation to occur. Very subtle, this. This kind of voice stays with the experience, but it directs it outward, rather than within. Remember that preacher who used to meditate on his passages of Scripture? (OK, it was me). He deflected by producing mini-sermons, but his own self, his own heart, remained untouched. He was too busy preaching out the truth to receive it himself.

Deflection is very subtle, but it may be the most common of the ways we tend to fail to have an experience at all. I was just talking with a friend who was singled out for an honour. A dinner was planned, an expensive gift bought, and the hall was packed. At the time, he enjoyed the experience, but as he said later, 'I wasn't fully in it, because I felt that if they only knew how lucky I had been to have made the scientific breakthrough they were honouring me for, they would be laughing in derision instead.' He took the compliment in a little, but then it was deflected out by a voice that told him, 'You've only succeeded because of luck.'

Negative voices are good at this. If someone has a voice that tells them they are unattractive, and they get a compliment about how nice they look, the sentiment flies in for a split second and then – boom – the deflector shield is raised and they say to themselves, 'They can't be looking too closely,' or, 'It's only because my clothes are expensive – they are not really complimenting me.' Positive voices, though, can help. I knew an author who would receive the compliment of a good review for maybe five seconds, or five hours, but he could never really stay there, because he was too fretful. 'They like this book, but will they like the next one I'm working on now?' And the besetting anxiety that drove him to achieve, sadly deprived him of any capacity to enjoy those achievements. The impending and impossible task served to deflect any possibility of tarrying with his deeper feelings of enjoyment.

ADD. Time for some familiar examples. Remember our four characters?

Defective Deborah

She's a dismisser. Now everything is her fault because her voice tells her she is defective, so that taints everything around her. That person didn't really like her, they were just pretending. That man who wanted her phone number, he's not interested in her – he's just a predatory male. She dismisses everything around her. She won't rate it. She dismisses anything that counteracts the voice. She interprets her whole world through the lens of this voice.

Get-Ahead Gerald

He's an absenter. He just can't turn up to life. He's shrunk it down to pure money-making. *Get rich or die trying* is in control. No surprise that most of his life he has been absent to the basic adventure of life, of raising kids, of being a husband, even enjoying the places he is blessed to visit.

Successful Sally

Remember her voice was to achieve the impossible or she felt a complete failure. She would dismiss anything that contradicted the idea that she was respected. She didn't have to live this way, but she did. She's a deflector – she might let something go in, for example her marriage was strong, but the good feeling from that was not allowed to transfer over into the rest of her world. It was only given partial power.

Never-Good-Enough Nigel

He's a deflector. Yes, something gets in; he has an experience in the Bible study. But ultimately it doesn't go deep because he's too busy making more resolutions to deserve the love of God – so he fails to actually receive it. A *Pharisaism* enters deep into the soul, and there are whole church cultures making us feel undeserving so that we will never have an experience of God.

That's how it works. That's ADD. That's how it steals our identity. Running and ruining our lives. Of course, there are other mechanisms of how our voices can take us away from ourselves. This is just one approach. But try it on for size. Pick two voices from the list you compiled, and ask how they might work to Absent, Dismiss, or Deflect you from a deeper experience of God and of life.

We are currently living through a great crisis of attentiveness. I read of a study in the USA that said that, on average, adults touch a mobile phone about 3000 times a day, and perform a minimum of 200 functions. This invention is out to attract us. Even when muted it can still vibrate. It's a great invention up to a point, but it can take us past the point of paying attention to the present, to what is in front of our noses, to who is sitting in front of us.

I'll never forget meeting the great theologian Lewis Smedes. He was coming up to his seventieth birthday and about to retire from full-time teaching. A group of students on the seminary campus where he taught took him out to lunch. 'What are you going to do in your retirement?' we asked, expecting him to talk about future book prospects. His reply staggered us: 'I'm going to work on relating to God *as a friend*.'

He said, 'I've always had a voice in my head when I relate to God. I suppose it comes from my Dutch Calvinist heritage and it has served me well. It was this: *Just trust and obey!* God was there to be served, rather than to be known. Maybe even behind this voice was another one, very Old Testament in its tone – don't get too close or I might have to injure you. It wasn't that I didn't enjoy the Christian life of course, but I have realised I have not enjoyed it as much as I perhaps could have. This voice kept me away from the more exciting idea that God could be known as a friend. I was missing out on the embrace of God. I will dedicate my retirement to that.'

I've never forgotten that admission. Smedes had been wonderfully productive for God, but for him to admit that after seventy years of pilgrimage he struggled to relate to God as a friend really impressed me, and convicted me. His 'trust and obey' voice had served to absent him from the place of enjoyment of God, or perhaps he had enjoyed God a little, but the voice came in to deflect his experience back out from enjoyment to duty, from intimacy to service.

Anyhow, we've got to get a sense of how our voices may be preventing us from turning up to our lives! If they do, they win. And life becomes a second-best activity. We settle into fantasies of really being someone else, or failing to have any strong experiences of anything much, or living out of an identity that isn't really us, and we end up a bundle of anxieties.

The good news is, though, voices don't just run and ruin, they can also renew . . . if we know how to deal with them.

6

How Voices Can Renew Us

TIME FOR HOPE. Time to believe that these voices can actually – in a perverse way – help us along to our deeper identity.

What is this deeper identity, however? What is the goal of life? What is a life well lived? I suppose that's a book in itself, but let's not get too hung up on it. For the Christian, at the very least the life we want is one that is centred on God, and not self-centred. We want a life that is lived out of a centre of gratitude to God, so that everything else becomes an overflow of that love we have received. That's basic, but profound.

And our voices are out to keep us self-centred. We might adapt the first principle of AA in this regard: *we admitted we were powerless over our voices, and our lives had become unmanageable.* When we still ourselves, we get a sense of how our voices might have been stealing our identity, pushing us into self-service rather than God-ward, even though we might have dressed it all up as sound Christian ministry.

More biblically, I love that verse in the Psalms as an ideal state for the Christian: 'What can I offer the LORD for all he has done for me?' (Psalm 116:12). That's the gratitude attitude, where we are so impressed at what God has done for all of us that we feel cosmically indebted to him, and all our being and doing is a response to that divine generosity, not in a craven or pressured way, but in a free and delightful way. That has to be the goal of life, right? To get to that upslope of gratefulness.

Actually, the person who first quoted that verse in my hearing was a very famous pastor in South Korea. It was his mantra, he said. And I do remember him talking about this individually (though I never heard him talk about this in a sermon). He was raised in North Korea, and when the war broke out he was able to flee to the south with his family. 'Up to then,' he said, 'I was a Christian who thought he was a squashed crumb that God had taken pity on.' But then he had a strange experience as he slept in the truck that was carrying him south on a dangerous road. 'I suddenly noticed a man beside me, dressed in the same kind of rags as myself. I had the overwhelming impression that this was Jesus. He said to me, "Will you build my Church?" I just looked at him, and then said, "Me – who am I?"' Then he seemed to wake up, and he began to answer that question. Who was he? One who had been called by Christ! That's who. Not a squashed crumb that could not be trusted. But a called pilgrim who could do the work of God. He said, 'From that moment, the call of Christ was upon me and I have lived my life since from that centre of awe and gratefulness – that he would call me to do his work.'

That's overflow.

I still think the best definition of the Christian life I ever heard was at a music festival over twenty years ago. A bishop was speaking. Can't even remember his name, and he was in a tent next to a raucous children's camp, so he was hard to hear. But this line I did get, and it's stayed with me like a mantra ever since: 'The Christian life is where we move from wondering to wondering.' Wondering at, since this world is full of impenetrable mysteries as well as staggering beauty, but also wondering why, since this world is also full of mystery and sadness, suffering and even horror. You move back and forth, always in a state of wondering, but always grounded in a God who gives replies if not answers. It's realistic. It's beautiful. It fits best the world as I experience it.

And experience is what we are talking about here. Voices are all about whether we can turn up and get a fuller experience of God and therefore of life or not. If they win, we don't. But since we can't get rid of them, how can they help? Yes, they are mostly designed to take us away from God, but we can change that. We can actually find that at least some voices can help us to God, and towards our deeper selves, rather than away from them.

Voices have great benefits. They can renew us. Voices that attack us can suddenly turn into forces that defend us, or assist us. They can help us find out *who we are*, and, knowing that, some of them can even help us find out *what to do*. The latter works negatively; that is, we have to do the opposite of what the voice is suggesting, and that may lead us to the better path. The former works positively, especially if we can still the rotten voices and hear the *Divine Voice*. But that takes great stillness and attentiveness.

Let me put it all up front as a proposition: *A voice is an invitation to define yourself as a group of love relationships, and not as a set of activities, or as a bundle of inadequacies.*

Whew. I'm glad that's out. Feels like childbirth. That's heavy. A set of activities? That's our positive voices. We define ourselves in terms of what we do, the roles we adopt. I'm a mother; I'm a lawyer; I'm a doctor; I'm a sportsperson; I'm a preacher; I'm a counsellor; I'm an evangelist. Not wrong but, in the deepest sense, not us either. A bundle of inadequacies? That's our negative voices. I'm hopeless; I'll never amount to anything; I am so unappreciated; I don't have it in me; I wish I was cleverer. Again, not us. They are all serving as false substitutes for our deeper selves, taking us away from being unique and filled up with the experience of being alive in this incredible world. They are snatching experience away from us.

This deeper self, this true self: what is it? It's just this: we are a relationship of love. That's our deepest identity as a person. Relationships with whom? Well, God first, and then everyone and everything else, from our spouse, to that bird, to our dog, to our community, to the oceans and mountains. We're back to the Eden blueprint. It never went away. It just gets lost sight of. We are a relationship because God is. God is a Trinity. A fellowship. So are we. That's what it means to be made in his image. From that *being* comes our *doing*.

Now voices actually help with this. They are *heretics for the truth*. Or, if you like, truth-producing errors. There is a lot of error in them, as we have seen, but if we know how to use them, they turn into gifts. Two gifts actually: *you are this*, and, *you are more*.

You Are This

A voice beckons you to the world of your deepest desires. It takes you down to the world of love.

I used to be amazed at how dull most preachers were. Then I read the sermons of St Augustine and saw why – they don't excite our deepest desires, as the great saint did. Not that every one of his sermons was a thriller. Sometimes he would speak for only five minutes, seeing that the people were too exhausted by the heat. Sometimes he would go on for two hours. But the more you read his sermons the more you get why he hit the mark. Augustine believed – with all the great doctors of the Church – that at our deepest level, *we are what we love.* In a sermon, he is out to put you in touch with your deepest loves (because most of us are out of touch with them), and direct that love to God. That's a successful sermon in the patristic era. Target: the loves of the heart. I suddenly realised that's why most modern preaching was so poor, because it was operating on a superficial level.

One type of preacher assumes that *we are what we know,* and so the sermon is basically giving us the information about a passage, doctrine or topic. Doesn't go deep enough. This probably came from Aquinas and the scholastic revolution in the twelfth century, and became turbocharged by the Reformation. But knowing the geography of Philippi or the thought of Barth does not make Scripture burn in the heart. As a great New York preacher of a bygone era – Harry Fosdick – once remarked, 'People do not come to church to learn the history of the Jebusites.'

Another type of preacher tries to be more emotional, because they assume that *we are what we feel.* So they deliver an emotional charge, maybe through great storytelling or whatever. But again, it keeps us superficial. We are not – at root – our feelings, but our loves, and when our loves are corrected, a true life can be lived, a true love relationship with God can take its place at the core of our being.

So a voice's first gift is to beckon us down to this layer of our deepest desires, because *we are what we love*. When we hear the voice 'I am so under-appreciated', think of the gift for a second. What is that voice really wanting, at the deepest level, at the love level? This voice tells us that we desperately want to be appreciated, to be loved. We want to be loved for who we are! But if we don't use the voice as a guide to our deeper self, it will keep us as a bundle of anxieties. *That email that came in this morning. He didn't refer to me by my full title. He doesn't respect me. Wait, he actually doesn't even care to figure out what I'm about or what I'm doing.* That's the voice taking charge and creating a rollercoaster of crisis after crisis. A person who is run by that voice is wanting to resign every three weeks because no one really cares. But if they can stop, take that famous 'grace hesitation' as Rowan Williams puts it, then they can ask, 'What is the deeper longing in the voice?' And then the voice becomes a shepherd, herding us down to our deeper identity, a love identity.

This works with a positive voice too. Take a person who is driven by the voice 'I am going to be the best banker in the world'. That voice defines the person as a financier out to maximise short-term profit for their institution through the financialisation of instruments. They are rich, often arrogant, and sometimes venal in the way they actually harm society by making the financial sector so fragile. Often a banker will say they have no choice but to adopt that template of effectiveness. Maybe so. Banking is a weird culture. People who have a so-called 'hole in their soul' are actually spotted and recruited according to Jonis Luyendijk, who wrote a book on banking personnel. Called *Swimming with Sharks*, his whole point was that the banking industry sets out to find people who need what is called 'extrinsic status' to feel good about themselves. This can be psych-tested, and the idea is to get people who have so little self-definition that they will do anything – literally anything – in order to please the group. They don't want someone who thinks for themselves. They don't want someone who will go against the herd. No, they are looking for a very smart human sheep. But the banking industry has, however, betrayed the deeper reasons for being a banker. What's the deeper beckoning underneath that voice? Surely it is to set people free, to help those who are struggling and give them the ability not to fret about their survival needs, or even to encourage them to build businesses of their own and create jobs for others. That's back to a love relationship with the people that matter, meeting them in their need, accepting their full dignity and raising them up to be all they can be. That's the deeper gift. That's what's underneath the voice. It's a gift . . . if we can pause long enough to attempt to go there.

I was once privileged to spend three retreats with two outstanding spiritual directors. 'Somewhere inside you there is another life, a potential self that wishes to emerge,' said one of them, 'and you will find this life, this self, by examining the substitutes of the false self.' Your voices are substitute identities, but their first gift – if we know how to take it – is to tell us where our heart is. You are this!

Did I say before that this isn't easy? Did I give the impression that this may take a lifetime? Yes, it's hard, but it is an adventure none the less. Everyone can take it. No one is excluded from this great inward and sacred adventure. We are trying first to get a sense of who we are before God, and to rest in the identity we are given, rather than the one we are anxiously striving to make. That's getting to 'Go'. Getting back to who we are is the essence of the spiritual struggle. Every good spiritual director will tell you that there are two forces at war within us – a death force that wants to take us away from God and ourselves, and a true or divine force that keeps drawing us to God and to our deeper identity. It's a battle. And I am characterising these forces in so far as they show up in voices.

And boy, do they! Perhaps we are all seeking to have a similar experience to Jesus at his baptism. He only heard the Divine Voice twice in his life, once in the river, once on the mountaintop (hey, that'll preach . . . get behind me, Preaching Voice). His ministry starts when he figures out who he is.

> . . . the heavens were opened and he saw the Spirit of God descending like a dove and settling on him. And a voice from heaven said, 'This is my dearly loved Son, who brings me great joy.' (Matthew 3:16b–17)

How about that for a start to one's ministry? It's a vision, I suppose, but it seems public at least in Matthew, since it says 'This is my . . . Son' as opposed to 'You are my Son' in Mark and Luke. It combines two Scriptures, Psalm 2:7 and Isaiah 42:1, together pointing to the identity of Jesus both as God's beloved Son and as the Suffering Servant who will be wounded for our healing. The curtains have been pulled back, and Jesus – and we – see who he really is.

The voice comes again when Jesus is taking a six-day retreat with Peter, James and John up a high mountain. The cross is looming. It's the so-called transfiguration scene, when the three disciples see Jesus shining in some form, along with Moses and Elijah. That quite excites them actually, and the ever-garrulous Peter suggests setting up three tents for them. Quite sensible in one sense – he wants to stay up there gazing at that glorious sight. Stuff the world, he is saying, let's make this a permanent ecstasy, just the six of us. But then they hear the Divine Voice. Much the same as before, with a little addendum that tells them they are not going to stay up there:

> . . . a bright cloud overshadowed them, and a voice from the cloud said, 'This is my dearly loved Son, who brings me great joy. Listen to him.' The disciples were terrified and fell face down on the ground. (Matthew 17:5–6)

Listen to him. Jesus is about to go and die. The world is only going to see a writhing, defeated-looking figure on a cross, but they have seen the Son of God glorified. They have seen his true identity, and their job for the rest of their lives will be to witness to that fact. But in the disciples' reactions I think we can see our own difficulties too. First, we are dazzled by the glory. Yes, meeting God at first seems great. Everything rocks along. But then, before long, we are confronted with our own helplessness when we see more of God, more than we bargained for. Peter babbles and burbles about pitching tents. But the crux is, when the voice speaks, they are terrified. It makes them drop to the ground 'terrified'. I suppose if there was ever something to shut Peter up, this was it. But why so scared? Because it is so terrifying. These men's ancestors begged Moses to hear God on their behalf: 'But don't let God speak directly to us, or we will die!' they said (Exodus 20:19).

It is a fearful thing to be addressed by the almighty God. But while they are prone, the Scripture says, 'Jesus came over and touched them. "Get up," he said. "Don't be afraid."' And when they wake, they see only him.

They get a touch. A physical touch. What a miracle is that! And my immediate response is, well, good for them, but I'll never feel a touch like that, since God isn't taking a human form on the earth as Jesus was at that moment.

But then, how many hands has Jesus got? That's the question, isn't it?

There's a line from a poem by e. e. cummings: 'No one, not even the rain, has such small hands.'

It's a line that sticks in your brain and you have to puzzle on it.

In a programme recently there was a vicar interviewed, who was suffering from motor neurone disease. He had only months to live and was in the final stages of being able to make himself understood. Soon it would be sign language until the end.

But his testimony was bright. The interviewer asked, 'How do you experience the love of Christ for you now?'

He said, 'Entirely through the loving hands of my wife who cares for me.'

So, in the light of this amazing passage, and this vicar's testimony, maybe we can change cummings's line: No one, not even the rain, has so many hands as Christ.

I suppose Christ ascended to make every Christian part of his body, and we can be touched by so many more hands now, and live out of his love for us, which gives us our deepest identity.

So don't long for a tent up at the summit. We'll get a golden tent soon enough.

But for now, feel the touch of Christ in the ordinary shadowland of life, through the hands of others who care.

And if we can develop the eyes to see this, maybe we will find life full of the most remarkable transfigurations.

Marilynne Robinson is one of the world's most feted novelists, and she does not hide her Christian faith. Asked if she had had any religious ecstasies, she said she hadn't. Did she hanker after them? 'A mystical experience would be wasted on me,' she said. 'Ordinary things have always seemed numinous to me.' And she went on to talk of that Vermeer painting, where sunlight falls on a basin of water in the hands of a serving woman, and yet the light shows a transfiguration of the ordinary.

It gets her by.

It could get us all by . . . if we remember to see how many hands Christ actually has in this world!

These hands will give us our deeper love identity. We are just trying to reach that point where we can say that prayer of Ignatius: 'I am from love, of love, for love.' Getting there may be a journey of terror. Christ's hands will help us. Our voices can actually be used to highlight our unmet desires.

Take them to Christ and we will find our deepest identity in a love relationship.

You are this, say the voices – but we can take the *grace hesitation* and let them lead us to our unmet desires, to that arena of experience and encounter where we might be able to hear the Divine Voice saying, *You are dearly loved*.

Well, it's a fight to get there, and there are some dark paths to tread. But we are invited to be part of an epic, not a French farce. Once we know who we are in Christ, and can sit there with some confidence, then the voices can help us again, and here we go on to their second gift: *You are more!*

You Are More

Remember we said that voices are heretics of the truth. The truth they are secreting to us is that the role they are offering is actually pathetic, a substitute, and we have to interpret them as saying, *You are more than this*.

It is worth going back to the temptations of Christ in the desert to see this in action. Jesus has had his '*You are this*' experience. He knows he is God's beloved Son. Right, but he is immediately tested to find out if he is the true Israel, which is why the desert experience lasts forty days to symbolise the forty years. Three voices are spoken to him. They all offer him false identities. But in the end – *through them* – he realises, *I am more*; he is able to vanquish the tempter and embrace his full ministry.

First temptation – turn these stones into bread. There's a little knife twist in the set-up, '*If*' you are the Son of God. The target is to create self-doubt that Jesus really is the beloved of God. Voices are all about identity wars. What's the idea here? Maybe it's this simple: just feed yourself. But what that does is shrink the work of the Messiah to a selfish satisfaction of hunger. Keep the work small. Become the world's most evolved person yourself. Jesus sees the fatal shrinkage of his identity right away. He is called to a ministry of epic proportions. He is universal. He's not here to feed people for a generation, but to put them in touch with God for all generations. Hence the rebuke: I'm going to live by every word that comes from the mouth of God. Big book, the Bible. Can't reduce it to one thing. God speaks many words, not just one. Jesus is going for the whole enchilada.

Easy to see how this repeats for us. It's a voice that tells us to be preoccupied with our own self-development, or our own church's story, and it won't allow God to beckon us out to a wider duty, or a wider role. Keep it small. Keep it modest. Keep it private. Reverse the suggestion, and you see the true dimensions of your ministry or call.

In a house church in rural Hunan I heard a great Chinese preacher. He put the Bible on a tree stump (yes, we were in the open air). All he said was this: 'I cannot tell you how important it is to realise that when one page of the Scripture is open, you must remember – you absolutely must remember – that all the other pages are closed. Thank you.' He sat down. There was a murmur that rose to a crescendo. He stood up again. 'Questions?' he barked. 'Erm, what the heck do you mean?' or words to that effect, came the question with some asperity. 'I mean,' he said, 'don't shrink the work of Christ's Church down to what he says now, to you, through this word . . . there's a lot more to come.' And then he added, 'If we really realised that, we would not have so much heresy around.' Jesus did the same to the devil. You are bringing the Bible down to satisfying hunger in one person, but the Bible is full of a greater call – how about satisfying the spiritual hunger of all people for all time?

Often a voice is trying to make us opt for something small. It's shrinking our ambition down. It's trying to keep it private, and probably irrelevant. Reverse it. *You are more.* That's the mantra.

It's the same process with the second temptation. Another 'If'. If you are the Son of God, chuck yourself off the roof of the temple and let the people see you parachuted down on the feathery wings of angels. Prove to yourself that you are the Son of God. See if the promises of God really work. Do spectacular works that the people will have to accept.

Now, always with a temptation, we have to play the game . . . *spot the identity substitution.* What's the identity the devil is really asking Jesus to live out of? It's the identity that ministry consists of spectacular deliverances – constant and public – otherwise you'll never really know if God is still with you, and you'll never really reach the people. See the bundle of inadequacies in there? How are you going to know God's still with you? You might have done a great miracle yesterday, but is he going to show up tonight? See the set of activities? You have to haul yourself everywhere, puff from city to city, and keep performing impossible stuff, and the more you do it, the greater the impact. If Jesus had set it up that way, he would have felt nothing but despair. Those great seven sign miracles in the first half of John's Gospel seem to close the people off to his message, not open them up. The signs dazzle, but they don't convict.

Jesus is clear. He doesn't need to do this stuff to prove God loves him. He can rest on the Divine Voice. He has received his deepest identity – beloved Son. He knows he enjoys the pleasure of the Father. He doesn't have to keep proving it. I *am more* than the repetition of miracles. And even more important, he gets that this way of proceeding is actually nothing to do with faith at all. We do not know how, when or where God will fulfil his divine promises. If we are always saying to God, 'You need to prove you are real by doing this miracle now,' we are putting ourselves in the place of God. He is our servant, not our Lord. And as Job found out, it's no fun trying to run the world by yourself, or understand it with your puny little brain. Let God be God.

I remember visiting a church that had a great revival in the early 1990s. I pitched up in 2010, and it was one of the saddest experiences of my life, because they were all pretending that they were still living in the early 1990s. They kept screaming for miracles. They laid on hands. They jumped about in pretend ecstasies. They told desperate stories of ongoing transformation. But you could tell God had moved on. The clock hadn't stopped, but they pretended it had. Only an outsider could see how sad it all was. Second temptation stuff. They were in charge, not God.

And the kingdom is harmed, because who wants to join a church where everyone pretends?

If only they could have said: *we are more than this*. More, even, than revival.

Third temptation. What's the game? Spot the identity substitution. No more 'Ifs', just a straight-up offer – worship me and get it all now! Everything. The world. The people. The glory. No need for all the sacrifice or the gore or the suffering. No need to wait. Get it all . . . now! Only one price to pay . . . count me in, says the devil.

I am more, says Jesus. Not that kind of messiah. He's being asked to be a different messiah. One that receives power from a lesser god, and uses a completely different means. He wants to be the kind of messiah who does things God's way, even if it takes longer, and involves blood and tears. Why? Because Jesus knows that a shortcut to glory cuts out the people he wants to save. Us! That's why God seems slow . . . because he's bringing us along. Shortcuts deprive us of the ability to grow. That's why Lent lasts as long as Easter.

Do you hear that voice that says, 'Come on, abbreviate the story here, cut out the toil and the suffering, and just roar straight to the victory'? So much of the global Church is mainlining on this. But no, we have to say, taking the slow walk to the cross is part of discipleship, if only because it puts God in charge, it makes change thorough, and it digni- fies us as we are given a chance to participate in bringing it about. Risky but beautiful. That's our God. That's why Jesus said, 'Get away, Satan. I'm going to be a messiah God's way, not yours, even if it costs my life.'

Identity wars, and worship wars. I suppose virtually all of life reduces down to these, like a minimalist painting. Identity wars – are we going to take our identity from the Divine Voice, and not our own? Worship wars – are we going to accept that God is in charge, and accept the mystery and the suffering, in the faith that this is the only and best way to live in fullness in this world and the next?

I'm grateful in my life for the witness of the persecuted church, who are always proving the value of this. Strangely, it's those individuals who don't see fruit in their lifetimes who give me the greatest hope. It fits somehow. We offer our lives to God in the belief that his will is done no matter whether we see it or not.

I remember visiting North Korea. Talk about worship wars! It's the most religious society in the world. On my first visit I was met by a guide who stepped forward and said, 'Welcome to heaven! You are now in the earthly paradise of Kim Il-sung. Come and see our paradise.'

I was whisked off to the opera. The performance began and an occasional translation in English was projected at the side of the stage. It became clear that the opera was about the great deeds of Kim Il-sung. It also became clear that the opera had been written by Kim Il-sung. Then one of the chorus lines was translated. It ran, 'Kim Il-sung gives eternal life to the Korean people for a thousand years.' OK, setting aside the dubious theology that makes eternal life last only for a thousand years, I thought to myself, 'What is such a religious concept doing in the mouth of such a materialistic communist?' As I was mulling this over, the opera ended with great fanfare, and suddenly a smiling face at least fifty feet high (of Kim Il-sung) was projected onto the back of the stage. Everyone jumped up from their seats and cheered wildly with their hands above their heads. I thought, 'Oh my, I've arrived on the pages of Orwell's *1984*.'

North Korea is the most communist society in the world, and also the most religious. The new god is Kim Il-sung's son, Kim Jong-il, and now joining the portly pantheon, Kim

Jong-un. They are said to have supernatural powers, and the whole society is a vast coercive network to force continual worship of these 'deities'. The worship is not subtle. You can see bands of schoolchildren laying offerings at the feet of huge golden statues of these figures at the centre of every town. Everyone is taught to revere them. Refuse, and the penalty is to rot in a camp that is a carbon copy of Auschwitz.

One day I was taken to an art gallery and shown a painting. It was called 'The Rout of the S.S. *General Sherman*'. It depicted a ship on fire, and Koreans with red trousers slaughtering those on board. My guide explained, 'This is when the ancestors of Kim Il-sung, our Great Leader, beat back the big-nosed Yankee imperialists who were coming to invade our land.' I fell into depression during this visit. All traces of the Church and God seemed to have been scoured from the land. There was a hatred of everything Christian, and I felt so sorry for the 22 million people of the country, cocooned from birth to death in this atheistic nightmare. I wondered how on earth God could establish his kingdom in such a place. It felt as though evil was in control, and nothing good could ever come of such a place.

A week later I was passing through Manila, and picked up a stray book on the history of the Bible Societies. I was flicking through the pages when my eye caught the phrase 'S.S. *General Sherman*' and I began to read the story of R. J. Thomas.

R. J. Thomas was a missionary to China in the middle of the nineteenth century. He had a heart for Korea, but it was a hermit kingdom even back then. No foreigners were allowed in. So he went to China instead, and bided his time. In 1865, the opportunity he had been waiting a lifetime for came along. An American ship, the S.S. *General Sherman*, was going to steam up the Taedong River to the capital Pyongyang in hopes of luring the Koreans into trade. Thomas bought a berth on the ship, hoping to meet some scholars in Pyongyang who spoke Chinese, and he took as many Chinese Scriptures with him as he could carry on board.

The trip was ill-fated. In a port on the way to the capital some of the *General Sherman*'s crew killed three Korean men in a bar-room brawl. When they reached Pyongyang the rumours had grown to such an extent that it was impossible to berth. The people of Pyongyang were convinced the foreigners had come for their children to make soup from their eyeballs. There was nothing to do but to turn around and head down the river.

Except they got stuck on a sandbank. Seeing them stranded, the Korean defence force lashed a series of small ships together, set them on fire, and they drifted to surround the *General Sherman*, which then caught fire. Everyone on board had to leap into the river. As they waded to shore they pulled out their swords, but were all clubbed to death by the waiting Koreans.

Thomas also waded to shore. Before he could speak, the club dashed his brains into the water. But his killer noticed he had not emerged with a cutlass, but brandishing books. He wondered if he had killed a good man, and picked up a couple of the sodden books.

Drying them off, he separated the leaves and saw that they were nicely printed. He could not read, but decided to paper the outside of his house with them, as was the custom at the time. Imagine his astonishment when he returned from the fields a few weeks later to find a clutch of long-nailed scholars earnestly reading his walls. One of these scholars became a Christian by reading a Gospel portion plastered into the wall. A small church started up and a relative of this first convert translated the New Testament into Korean a generation later.

Yet Thomas never lived to see the fruit of his labour. In fact, as the club swung towards his brow, he may well have thought the trip had been a tragic mistake. I wonder if his final voice was, 'Oh no, what a terrible mistake I have made.' He died, his life's purpose unfulfilled, his potential unrealised. For all aware of Thomas's death, his life was a mystery for years afterwards.

But his life was not in vain. The meaning of life does not consist in what we make of it, but in what God makes of it. Even evil can serve God and make a way – a bit like the devil in the desert. When we yield our lives to Christ, he makes us living stones, part of an eternal kingdom constructed on the cornerstone of Christ Jesus himself (1 Peter 2:1–9). Success is not about achievement then, or what we make of ourselves. It's about placement, or what God makes of us.

So instead of obsessing about what our life's purpose is – as so many do today in the Western Church, while seeking to control the future – I have to take the lesson from the persecuted church that it is OK to die quite unaware of our life's meaning. We can rest in trust that God, in his mercy, has made us a 'living stone'. The tempter always smiles when we fast track.

This is how God builds the kingdom. And what is remarkable is that it is ordinary people who, through the grace of

God, bring great changes. The sheer dramatic effrontery of it takes my breath away. It's perfectly captured in these wonderful verses in Psalm 118:

> The stone that the builders rejected has now become the cornerstone.
> This is the LORD's doing, and it is wonderful to see.

God takes the rejected things of the earth, and builds his eternal kingdom from them.

Our voices. If we still them, we can hear, *you are this!* If we can rest in that, the voices can also be reversed, as we say to them, *we are more!* Jesus knew the kind of messiah to be. Now he knew how he was going to wield power, prestige and privilege. The voices actually helped clarify his activity after the Divine Voice clarified his identity.

That's how the voices can renew our lives, rather than just ruin them. God has made a way.

Now it's time to see how we can deal with these voices.

The five ways . . . coming up.

Relax. You don't need all of them. You might just need one or two of them.

But if you don't have at least one, how are you going to hear from God who you really are, and find your way to what you really should do . . . even if you never understand it?

Sounds like following God to me!

7

#1 Talk Back to the Voice

So we have got to the point where we have stilled enough to know who the voices are, and have named them and realised their power; now it's time to deal with them. All that follows is a toolbox of *five major ways* to stop the voices ruining your life. Use them, and our voices – some of them at least – might well help remake us. And be warned – one tool may not be enough. If voices cluster and gang up on us, so our tactics need to gang up on them.

The first tactic is blindingly obvious: TALK BACK TO THE VOICE!

Strange that much of the raw emotional power of a voice relies entirely on our refusal to contest it. Talking back to a voice only takes a moment, but it can defang a voice very effectively. A voice has a 'Wizard of Oz' quality. The wizard is a fraud. And so – especially with the negative voices – is the voice terrorising you.

But what does it mean to talk back to it? Something so obvious cannot be easy. The essence of this idea is to dispute the effect of the voice. Most negative voices run on exaggeration. OK, try these steps.

1. Still, notice and name

This is preparatory to all tactics. We need to dial down, tune in to the noise, and target the voice that is having such an impact. We often notice a voice by its traces – its feelings. I remember flying half way around the world to speak at some very impressive conferences. I sat in the hotel room gazing at my notes, and felt such a deep dread at the prospect of speaking before so many people. It was as if a dark blanket covered my soul. I felt sick, and my hands shook when making myself a coffee. It was even hard to get up and move around.

This was a voice. Name it. OK, I called it Disaster Voice. It said, 'You are going to make an almighty mess-up. You are going to let everybody down. Everyone's going to be disappointed. It will be a disaster.' And the voice came so fast, so insistent, so strong, that depression fell like a hammer on my heart. There was no time to contest the conclusion, and all I experienced was the feeling.

2. Argue back

But I was also angry. This voice was taking away my peace, my hope, my equanimity. It was turning the trip away from something to enjoy into something to dread, something broken. I didn't want to continue to experience this awful dread anymore. Being nervous, yes, that's one thing, but this blackness, this terror, no, that was something much worse.

So I talked back. But you have to talk back a certain way, and that is to dispute the voice, not to ask for confirmation. If you say, 'Well, show me the ways this is going to be a disaster,' you are just asking the voice to enter the pulpit and sermonise. The voice will give you plenty: people won't listen; people will be bored; people will be offended; and on and on. That kind of dialogue makes it worse, because we are giving the voice an echo chamber.

No, the key to talking back to the voice is to contest the point the voice is making. 'Wait a minute, why will this inevitably be such a disaster? I've got God on my side. Most people want to learn and are coming to give me a fair hearing. I know I can hold their attention because I have been invited as a good speaker – they know how I sound.' Warm to it. Let the voice have it. 'Hey, the stories I am going to tell, they are world-beaters. They will never have heard of that person, and her story is so heart-rending, and so transformative, it will work.'

Of course, Disaster Voice has its comebacks, like, 'Yes, well, that may be a great story, but you are trying to do this for God, and God knows what a hypocrite you are, so it will fall flat.'

But you keep contesting back. 'I may be a hypocrite, sure, but you are not correct that God will punish them through me. He will honour the person whose story I am telling, even if the mouthpiece has not been as holy as he should be.'

And the more you do this the more it leads to the deepest part of it all.

3. Expose the lie

Negative voices are usually lies at their root. They are wrong. So I said, 'Wait a minute, you say this is going to be a disaster, but it's crazy to say no one will like me, or I'll never hold their attention.' And the more you talk back and dispute the voice, the more you realise that the voice is really spewing out complete bunk. It's lying. It's not true. And you are being rendered joyless over something that is just not going to happen. And as you talk back, disputing the disaster scenarios, something happens. The voice gets smaller. It's as if this type of voice is a huge growling bear in the shadowy corner of the room. That's its power. It mutters in the shadows where you cannot see it. But when you bring it out into the light, it's not a giant dangerous bear at all; it's just a gibbering, mischievous little monkey.

4. Call its bluff

Allow the voice to set out the scenarios. Call the voice's bluff. 'OK, even if you are right, and I make no impact, why is that a disaster? I'll just chalk it up to experience and move on. My wife will still love me. My kids will still adore me. My job is still safe.' And so on. I've noticed something about lies – the most powerful ones are blatant and vague. This disaster voice never really specifies what the disaster will be like, or makes it so vague that everything qualifies. For example, it's a disaster if no one listens, but it's a disaster also if everyone listens but no one does anything. Or it's a disaster if people react negatively, but it's a disaster if they all just agree. Clever that . . . because everything that happens seems to certify the truth of the lie.

Call its bluff. Follow the voice's dire warnings, and satisfy yourself that the things you are being emotionally pulled into dreading, are not actually worth dreading at all.

I've seen this at work among the persecuted church. Persecutors tell the most blatant lies about the Church, because the more blatant they are, the more incapable they are of falsification. I remember Hindu extremists in India putting about the lie that Christians were Trojan horses for the Vatican and the CIA. Crazy. But it was believed. Then an Australian missionary, Graham Staines, was burned alive in his jeep with his two small sons by Hindu extremists. He was a simple man who just wanted to help leprosy victims, and had worked in India for many years. How could the lie apply to him? Actually, it worked perfectly. Because there was so much international outrage about the grisly killings that the Hindu extremists were able to turn round and say, 'See, we told you . . . the international community would not be so upset if they were not using the missionaries to take over India.' A lie so blatant, so vague, so odious, has more power than a clever one, because almost everything that happens subsequently seems to confirm the truth of it. We're on Himmler territory here.

5. Confront the lie with the truth of your experience

Perhaps the most important power element in speaking back to the voice, though, is to argue from your own store of experience. I was fortunate to receive spiritual direction from a great master of the art, and he once said that his biggest conclusion, after fifty years of helping people find a more sacred dimension in their lives, was this: *few people rate their own spiritual experience!* No wonder, perhaps, surrounded as we are by books and stories designed to make us covet some-one else's experience, until we think our own walk is thin and dull by comparison. No, said the spiritual director, everyone has been given a great treasure of experience with God; the great task of the spiritual life is to rate it and draw upon it.

Remember, talking back to a voice is to engage in reality wars. The voice is trying to lure us into an area of unreality. It doesn't want us to live in the real world of now. So it is out to spin an alternative, and frequently catastrophic, view of the universe, which bears little resemblance to the real world. I had a friend who struggled with a cocaine addiction. A city high-flyer whose main addiction was to pressure and dead-lines, he could only function if there was a crisis. He was paid very highly because he could really deliver in these conditions. But out of this came a sad dependence on a line of cocaine at lunchtime in the executive washroom to give him the ups to face the afternoon trades. His voice was simple: 'We need to feel really buzzed to be confident that we can make a million today!'

One day, after a poor run of trading, he sat down and began to marshal evidence on a sheet of yellow paper. He computed the value of his trades when he knew (and only he knew) he had been high on cocaine and when he had not. He never told his employers, but his trades were three times as profitable without the white powder as when he was snorting it. In fact, the cocaine made him reckless, and inclined to take bigger risks than he would normally be comfortable with. He went into his office, shut the door, and placed his cocaine powder on a chair opposite him, and began to dialogue with this voice that had driven his professional life for the last five years. 'Look, the figures don't lie . . . you make me miscalculate risk . . . you are too expensive personally . . . I feel less connected to the real world with you than without you.'

And so on. The more he talked, the more the voice grew smaller. The bear lost its deep growl and the monkey came gibbering into the room.

He was free. Now, it wasn't quite that simple. There was the not-so-small matter of the chemical dependency on the cocaine to overcome, but he was smart enough to get help on that.

But this is the key to it. The most powerful evidence we can marshal against a voice is the reality of our own experience. That's a reality that you can trust, but you have to pull it up and value it. A voice will always run from a testimony of the real world.

I suppose the point is, when you access your own truth in response to the voice, you have no doubt that your own experience is true. It has the force of truth.

It's not easy. None of these tactics is. Sometimes it is easier to see the world through cocaine-tinted lenses. In Somerset Maugham's masterpiece, *Of Human Bondage*, the central character gives in to a voice and starts to descend into a dreadful addiction. Maugham's narration goes:

He did not know that thus he was providing himself with a refuge from all the distress of life; he did not know either that he was creating for himself an unreal world which would make the real world of every day a source of bitter disappointment.

Such a great sentence and it gets to the heart of addiction. Think of porn. Its great danger is to create an unreal world so that the real world becomes a disappointment, and what a tragedy that is, because the real world is beautiful and full of grace. The tragedy of an addiction is that it blinds us to the beauty of the world we all live in and have access to, and creates an exhausting stampede for what we can never have. So speak back to the voice, and value the experience of the real world over an unreal world.

But what makes us speak back?

Personally, I think it's desperation. You just reach a point when you get fed up. Perhaps you see the consequences of being in thrall to the voice, and you don't want to keep going down that road. Often this desperation is caused by an event. An alcoholic may realise they have a problem only when a spouse walks out, or they commit a gaffe that loses them their job. And another voice finds itself, replacing 'I need another drink to feel good' with 'If I have another drink I'll lose everything'.

This particular tactic is similar to Cognitive Behavioural Therapy, which is where a person is taught to contest negative thoughts so that they don't morph into negative feelings. Say there is an event – your boyfriend has been seen kissing another woman. Suddenly you have a thought about that:

'Oh no, I'm not good enough for him. What am I doing wrong that he is not satisfied with me?' And that leads to the feeling of sadness and lack of self-worth: 'I'm not attractive and I'm so angry and sad that I can't trust him anymore.' CBT is where a person gets help to think differently about the trigger event, which will also lead to a different feeling.

So the boyfriend has betrayed you. What about reacting differently? 'Perhaps he just had too much to drink?' And you refuse to feel betrayed. Or another thought: 'If he did that, we are not as well suited as I thought we were . . . time to move on and be happier.' Anyway, you see it's the same idea. It is the refusal to let the voice have free rein. You drop off automatic pilot, and say, 'I could think about this differently,' and you refuse to allow the destructive voice to have a monopoly of interpretation over the trigger event.

CBT, of course, doesn't always work, and the practitioner often needs help to accomplish it, since it isn't easy to break down an automatic process that flashes by at the speed of thought. But that's OK. That's why we need a range of tactics to come at our voices. It's a package, not a silver bullet.

A voice uses a distinct rhetorical device, which we see all the time in the rather diseased world of political discourse today. It's called proleptic, where you take an imagined future scenario and present it as current reality. Mark Thompson, the former Director General of the BBC, highlighted what he regarded as an example in his book *Enough Said: What's gone wrong with the language of politics?* When the Affordable Health Care for America Act was being proposed under the Obama administration, the Republican 'Tea Party' politician Sarah Palin posted on Facebook a phrase that would bring a lot of heat and opposition to the bill. The phrase was 'death panel'. The origin of the term was hers, though the concept had come from some serious misrepresentation of the bill, which in an early draft form offered end-of-life counselling sessions to patients. But the phrase 'death panel' went everywhere, and people just got bounced into assuming that Obamacare meant compulsory panels sitting on even able-bodied people and trying to coax them into terminating their own life. But what power it had. Thompson writes:

> A phrase which exaggerated and distorted a claim that was itself false, and which in any event had virtually nothing to do with the central thrust of Obamacare, had changed the course of politics. In fact, it is probably the only thing that many Americans can recall about the whole health-care debate. As the veteran conservative firebrand Pat Buchanan remarked about Sarah Palin: 'The lady knows how to frame an issue.' (*Enough Said*, p.5)

Thomson may be overegging it, as there are rather terrifying death panels in some western countries, but the point is made that a voice is very good at passing off a prejudice for a fact. I was reading a great book recently by one of my favourite social commentators, who archly slid in the line, 'Of course, since religion cannot be true, we have to find a more compassionate way.' That sentence did a lot of work. Not only the false claim that religion is by definition untrue, but that religious people lack compassion. In my experience, the more vinegary the writer, the more they attempt to pass their prejudices off as universal truths – perhaps they don't get challenged enough.

Anyway, a voice has the same skill. It knows how to frame an issue, and leave the most important stuff to be dealt with outside the frame. And as we have seen, it relies on its speed. It takes an event, it distorts it, and bang – before you can draw your next breath – you are having an emotion that is entirely illegitimate. That's why *still, notice and name* is our lifeline – it gives us the opportunity to contest. Take it, and live.

One last thing. Have hope, because calling the voice's bluff can be a devastatingly effective exercise, even if it seems rather naff and simple on the surface. That great servant of the persecuted church, Brother Andrew, was meeting with leaders of the church in Indonesia. Persecution was picking up, some churches had been burned, a few pastors chased from their homes by mobs who had torched their homes. They were very discouraged when they met him. He saw this and then began to talk to them with a simple question.

'OK, you have had some trouble. What's the worst that could happen to you next?'

The pastors thought about this. 'We could get arrested.'

'Then what's the worst that could happen to you?'

They discussed some more. 'We could get beaten in jail.'

'And then what's the worst that could happen to you?' pressed Andrew.

'We could get tortured very painfully.'

Andrew said, 'OK, and then what is the worst that could happen to you?'

They thought long and hard. 'We could die from the torture. Terrible, lingering deaths, during which we might divulge anything they asked.'

Andrew smiled at them. 'And then what's the worst that could happen to you?'

They stared at him, and as it dawned on them the mood began to lift. 'We would be released from our suffering and enjoy unmediated fellowship with Jesus Christ for all eternity.'

A bit drastic maybe, and not for everyone. But it was the right antidote to their voice of fear, and persecuted Christians get to that point with great regularity.

Talk back to that voice, the voice that is making you ill, depressed, sad, angry, stupid. The chances are, it's a liar.

Speak back to it the right way, and live.

8

#2 Befriend the Voice

I HAVE A LOVE-HATE relationship with St Augustine. For nigh on eight years the man's writings sat on my chest like an elephant, constricting creativity and life itself as I struggled to get a nodding acquaintance with his five-million-word corpus in order to finish a PhD. Many times I despaired of ever saying anything coherent about the man's thoughts, much less convincing two academics that I had made a unique contribution to the vast one-thousand-year industry of Augustinian studies. I hated him for a while, and also my supervisor who had put me on to him in the first place. I still count my greatest emotion as when, after passing my viva and hearing those sweet words, 'minor corrections only', I was in the Oxford Blackwells bookshop a few months later and spied a new tome on Augustine. At first my heart sank. This tome was important. Weighty. Its width grinned at me as if to say, 'Hee, hee, you thought you were finished. Well this will blow it all off course' (yes, finishing a PhD is equivalent to war trauma). Then suddenly it hit me; I was finished. Manuscript handed in. Passed. A wave of joy swept over me from head to toe, so intense it prickled my scalp. 'I don't have to read it,' I shouted. I started laughing. 'I don't have to read it,' I shouted again, shocking the calm of the Norrington Room. Everyone thought I was a loon. I was. I admit it. Totally.

After that near nervous breakdown, Augustine gave me a huge gift despite his penchant for sitting like an elephant on my chest. It's this: in ministry and in life, you make no progress if you do not first descend to the level of your deepest desires, from which we are all estranged at first. You have to go there first to make any forward progress as a person, as a Christian. And that is the territory we are in when we talk about befriending a voice.

And yes, folks, that insight was worth eight years of toil, and maybe upwards of thirty grand in fees.

Every time Augustine started a sermon, he keyed in to our deepest desires. The modern preacher tends to assume that *we are what we know*, and they give you all the info and intel about the passage. Nonsense. When did knowing the truth actually cause us to change human behaviour? Another group of preachers assume that *we are what we feel*, and are out to give you an experience through great storytelling. Again, way off the reservation. When did an emotion launch a new resolve? Augustine said – and he was right in a way we have totally forgotten – that *we are what we love*! Something has gone wrong with our loves, our desires, he says, and every sermon of his starts by accepting that we are in some way 'away from ourselves' as the Scripture describes the poor Prodigal Son among the pigs. Only when the prodigal son 'comes to himself' does he head back to his father, and that wonderful embrace.

But coming back to ourselves on the deepest level of our desires is not easy, because we don't live on that level. In fact, we live in a world that is always pulling us away from them, and offering superficial solace. Augustine says, with his deceptive simplicity, that there are only two problems: either you desire the wrong thing, or you desire the right thing too much! That's where humans have gone wrong. Since the beginning of time. And today. And, no doubt, tomorrow.

Example. Take apartheid in South Africa. What was wrong with it? Just this: over-love. A group of whites loved the land *too much*. So much that they couldn't share it with anyone else, including the black majority. That over-love turned into a vicious fear that tore Africa's most advanced society apart. Mandela was so smart not to love the land too much – it had to be shared, and a bloodbath was averted. It's a shame that some of his successors have not shown the same awareness.

Anyway, where are we going here? Befriending the voice is the second tactic we might have to use to deal with our voices, but it requires us to work at the level of our deepest desires. That's hard. Befriending the voice means looking down into it, touching the pain behind the voice, acknowledging the good the voice is trying to give us, tuning in to the deeper longing in the voice, and – eventually – giving ourselves that deeper longing.

Augustine-type territory.

Sorry.

Maybe this is why therapy often becomes so helpful to us in this area. We may need someone else to help us descend down the ladder to the realm of our deepest desires.

But the key insight is not astonishing and certainly not unknown, and you can find it in a thousand self-help books: many a negative voice within us that paralyses us now, started life as a good voice outside us that just wanted to spare us embarrassment. Great intentions. Disastrous consequences.

You've probably come across it before, in books like *Embracing Your Inner Critic*, a helpful guide to dealing with the more critical voices in our lives. Here's how it might work. A friend at university was an atheist. That was fine as far as it went. He had his life and I had mine. The problem was that he was a vicious and abusive atheist. On any other topic he was relaxed and charming. But if the talk drifted to religion, he would undergo this Jekyll and Hyde change. His face would darken and redden, his breathing would quicken, his voice would become shrill and angry and he would start shouting. He didn't lose his poise. He had a litany of accusations he would reel off against religion, and many of his beefs were perfectly fair – massacres of innocents in the name of religion in western Europe following the Reformation; the Spanish Inquisition; Catholic cardinals in Africa depriving AIDS sufferers of condoms; Pakistani mullahs urging Taleban to kill young females who want to go to school, and so on, and so on, and this was before 9/11. But you wondered, 'Why the sneer?' And why the utter inability to accept that religion might have a good side as well as a bad side? Religion is the greatest provider of schools and hospitals the world has ever seen, and shatters the tribalism that only looks after your own and that so tears up the world. But no, you couldn't put any counter-arguments to him. He just got more and more vicious.

Well, as a great Cambridge academic, John Bowker once wrote that God gives us the right to avoid him, and my friend was taking advantage of that right. But that all changed one night. He came to my room a very chastened person. It seemed that his sister was considering becoming a nun. Her story was astonishing. She had run away, got into drugs, and worked as a prostitute in Bristol's red light area. But now she was clean because a group of Christians had surrounded her, given her support, and even fought a court case so she could claim damages against her pimp. He said to me sadly, 'I was so angry, but now I'm just sad, because I have to admit that religion can do some good.'

I stared at him. 'Why is that so hard to admit?'

He replied, 'Because my dad always told me that religion screws you up, and religious people will always keep trying to evangelise you, and you've got to be free of that.'

I said, 'Well, we've all heard your father's voice coming through you all right. You go apoplectic if anyone suggests religion could do anyone any good.'

'That's because of what my father went through, and only admitted on his death bed,' he said. His father had been raised a Catholic, and was sent to a fine public school in Ireland. But he suffered sexual abuse there, by a priest, and his letters home detailing the abuse were not believed. Not surprisingly, he reacted against the faith and professed a fierce and sometimes violent communism until his dying day. My friend said, 'When he warned me about religion, I suppose he was just trying to make sure I never fell into the clutches of abusive priests – he wanted what was best for me; he wanted me to make my own way.'

Then he said, 'I guess I internalised his voice too much. He just wanted me to think for myself and not accept religious answers on trust, but that voice lost its boundaries, and somehow I ended up with a voice that carried all my father's bitterness, and told me all religion is evil. But I can't carry that bitterness anymore. I have to accept that religion can be good – my sister is clean, thanks to faith-filled people, not the local branch of the Communist Party.'

Perhaps it was the whisky, but he decided to celebrate the breaking of his father's anti-religion voice by drop-kicking Ludwig Feuerbach's *The Essence of Religion* – the text which Marx assumed debunked religion – around my room. Yes, it was a very intellectual form of exorcism, but it proved permanent in its effects. He became a doctor for a Christian charity. To this day he is not a believer, but he is respectful of religion and the good it can do, so much so that he contributes to it himself. To work for a Christian charity would have been impossible with his father's voice in control.

That's an example of how a controlling critical voice was originally out to do good. My friend's father just wanted his son not to be abused, or fall under the influence of religious manipulators. But the voice burst its banks and became this angry voice that kept squawking, 'All religion is evil; all religion is evil.' When he was able to see this, and where the voice had come from, he was able to soothe it, defang it, and release himself from the grip of its extreme bitterness and fear.

There may be many voices like this, and they don't all have to come from a parental voice that was out to spare us pain and embarrassment. But it pays to notice that some voices do have – at their root – a kind intention. Befriending that element can shatter the power of the voice.

So what does it consist of to befriend a voice like this? How about these four steps.

Step One: Touch the pain behind the voice

Underneath, the voice may have come from a pain that we experienced. Try and trace the voice back to when you first heard it. Was it in an exam that you first heard that voice, 'You'll never succeed'? How about the sports ground? Was that when you first heard, 'You're useless'? Or was it in an embarrassment in a love relationship that you first heard, 'You're not attractive at all – who do you think you are kidding?'? It's not that this voice was spoken out to you, but you spoke it to yourself. Access the pain within. That's important because it creates compassion, and that is compassion you are going to show to yourself. But first, just see and feel the destruction that the voice has wrought. It's OK, sit in the dark for a bit. If you want to shed a tear, go ahead. That nine-year-old had no business having that pressure piled on them.

One very athletic lady overheard a male friend say about her as a teenager, 'She's really hot if you just put a bag over her head.' Braces, contact lenses and a skin condition cured and she was a knockout ten years later, but she hung her head as if she wanted a balaclava over it. Go back to that pain. Only from there can a better way perhaps be found – to accept her looks but not to be so attached to the exhausting 'game' of looking attractive for the opposite sex.

Step two: Acknowledge the good the voice is trying to do

That voice that says, 'Don't have any emotions.' Remember, that's probably coming from a protective parent who didn't want us to have our heart broken all the time. It might have started out as something like, 'Don't give your heart away too quickly.' Accept that the voice is trying to help. One might even say back, 'OK, thanks for your input. It's kind of you to be worried about me being devastated, but you can back off now, because it's a bit silly not to feel anything, isn't it?' So many of these voices are what are called 'truth-producing errors'. Parental voices are very like this. Maybe all the voice wants is to avoid us getting into a situation where we will experience pain or embarrassment. What's gone wrong is how the voice is phrasing it. Parental voices might have been harsh, but the chances are 'You're just a fake' started off as 'Don't take on that task or role before you grow up a bit more, then you'll be ready.' So thank the voice for its concern, then politely tell it that it needs to go back behind the ropes. It is a help up to a point, but it has no business assassinating your character.

Step three: Tune in to the deeper longing of the voice

Remember what we were saying about our deeper desires, our more primal loves? Tease out that there is a deeper longing in that critical voice. 'Don't feel anything or you'll just embarrass yourself' covers a real desire to be in a relationship, and to accept that loving involves losses as well as joys. Or, 'I really wish I could express my emotions and meet someone there.' Or, 'I really do want to be vulnerable and be hurt because I want to be in a relationship. I am longing for someone to meet me there.' Part of the counselling process is to help a client re-parent themselves, to make sure they give themselves what they never received. You are learning to do that for yourself.

Step four: Gift yourself that deepest longing

What would be one kind thing that you can give to yourself to meet that longing? 'You didn't greet me with a kiss,' Jesus says to the Pharisees when the prostitute anointed his feet with expensive ointment and kissed his feet (Luke 7:45). Such a poignant phrase, since Jesus probably as an adult received very little physical affection. We would do well to 'kiss this voice' and gift ourselves the deepest longing. If we are longing for relationship, give ourselves the gift of a weekend away in the company of interesting people. If we are longing for acceptance, arrange to join a club of some sort and begin to belong. If we are longing for a bit of peace and quiet in a crazy life full of demands, it's time to say no, go away, take a retreat, and see if the world will stop turning. Underneath this voice is a longing.

This is hard work. Inner work. Getting down to these layers of ourselves, and peeling away what really lies behind voices like 'You're mean', 'You look dreadful', 'You're too short,' 'You're too tall', 'Don't open your mouth . . . you'll just bore everyone' often takes a professional companion, like a therapist or a spiritual director. But no one is asking you to fight your voices alone. Conscript as much help as you can. It's worth it.

I think this is probably the most complex and difficult strategy in dealing with the voices, so it's probably worth going through the four paradigmatic characters introduced earlier and seeing how this process of befriending works in practice for them.

GET-AHEAD GERALD

He wondered why he was so driven to just make money. He realised he had got this from his parents, as they were poor immigrants, and they pushed him to succeed significantly so he could look after them in their old age. That was the world they had come from – the world of an agricultural village where your only pension was an able-bodied son. So he said, 'My crazy drive came from a good place – it was a good reason, they just wanted the best for me and to be looked after in their old age.' So he sees where it started. It's a good family. A good Italian family. But then he thought, what do I do with this now? Well, they are dead. I don't need to look after them anymore. I don't need to please them. So I will go back to the gravesite and thank them for their attitude. That was his gift. And as he did, the ritual took the power of the voice away. It was, you might say, a sacrament of thankfulness that closed the door.

SUCCESSFUL SALLY

'If I don't achieve the impossible, I'm a failure,' she said. She recognised it was her father's voice. Some of the time she saw he was trying to appreciate her, but he couldn't say so – he was just too inarticulate in a way a lot of fathers still are. But he felt he was being a good parent by insisting she should not settle for mediocrity: 'Don't be average.' Underneath, he was really saying, 'Because you're better than average.' Now it wasn't until after her breakdown that she really put that together. The pain of that was not good, because her father would hurt her, and ignore her, in order to enforce that attitude. But she also saw that this was his way of showing that he loved her. His own life had been one of thwarted ambition. He died when she was just in her thirties, and she had her breakdown in her sixties. Underneath, there was a love in it. But what she really longed for her father to say was, 'You're good enough . . . well done. I'm proud of you.' So she began to say this to herself. One day, she plucked up the courage to ask a group of friends to write something positive about her for an upcoming birthday. One of them described her as a 'well-made quiche'. Her one kind thing was risking allowing someone to write that, and take it in. So it stopped ruining her.

NEVER-GOOD-ENOUGH NIGEL

Remember his voice was, 'Whatever you do, it will never be good enough.' 'Where did that voice come from?' he asked.

It was from his parents and his school teachers. No problem accessing the pain – he would get walloped if he didn't get a good enough grade in art, or maths, or spelling. But as he sat with this, he could see that his parents were just trying to make sure he would not be disappointed and were showing him that if you are going to succeed you are going to have to work hard. 'It won't just come to you,' they were in effect saying. They were getting him ready for life and its hard knocks. They just wanted to make him ready for the world. So that was why they had instilled this voice inside him. But what would be the kind thing he could give himself? He decided he would join an improvisation amateur theatre company. Why was that a kind thing? Because it broke the power of the voice – this was something you did that you could not prepare for. That was the point. You had to learn to be happy being unready, or ready for absolutely anything. That's a different way of working. So he would get out on stage with other actors, and lift off from the suggestions of the audience. Brave. Terrifying. And so healing, because he was putting himself in a situation where the lie in the voice, 'You don't know enough' was rendered untrue in real life. The improvisation worked . . . from his spontaneous wits.

DEFECTIVE DEBORAH

Her voice was 'When anything goes wrong, it's my fault'. Accessing the pain also took her back to her family. The father was uninterested. She wanted him to help her with her homework, but he was tired and blew his top. So she learned that if she wanted peace, better just placate Dad.

Everything was blamed on her. But she could see that the voice was trying to protect her from her father's explosions, and he was teaching her self-sufficiency to compensate for his own lack of joy. So she did find that the voice worked for her. The deeper longing of the voice, though, was to feel that the world is not always cruel, and she just wanted someone to be present to her and accepting of her even when something would go wrong. So she took action. She noticed when she would absent herself in conversations or conflict, and deliberately allowed herself to be present to a struggle. Once, when she was organising something very important, certain key people took umbrage and were about to bow out. But she went to them and shared, 'I know you have a genuine concern here, but you know, I really would like you to be here. I absolutely value you here.' To her astonishment they stayed. Stayed because they actually liked her. That set her on the road to healing.

It's not easy dealing with your voices. I remember having a horrible voice. I identified it as, 'You'll never make the grade.' No matter what I achieved, there was always this nagging voice saying, 'Yes, but will that do it?' I struggled to take any sense of peace or fulfilment from any achievement.

I must say I never really got this until I ended up having a few sessions with a Jungian therapist. I began to realise that much of my anxiety came down to a time when I failed an important exam. It was called the 11-plus. You took it in the UK at the tender age of ten or eleven, and frankly whether you passed or not determined whether you went on to a grammar schools and became a professional, or you went to a secondary modern school and became a steel welder or a joiner. It was the exam that society used to separate white- from blue-collar workers, and many believe it was a disgrace that the educational system was set up in that way then. It's better now, thank God, although I think the grade anxiety seems to be even worse today, but there is less at stake.

I failed it, which meant I was destined for the secondary modern. I was quite unaware of the professional long-term consequences, but what was terrifying was that all my friends from primary school would be going to the grammar schools, and I would be going to a rough secondary modern, believing that I would get picked on and beaten up by a rough bunch of kids who had no interest in learning about anything except violence.

As fate would have it, a well-off man intervened, and said he would pay for me for one year to go to a grammar school, and if I 'passed my review' (as it was ominously termed) I could stay on in the school as a non-fee-paying student. This was generous in the extreme, as my parents had no resources to pull off such a scheme by themselves. The trouble was, the pressure was on, and here's the rub . . . *nobody told me what the grade was!* What did one have to do to pass this elusive review? When I got 60 per cent on my English score, was that too low, or was it acceptable? When I got 85 per cent for RE, I still couldn't rejoice – maybe the bar was set at 90 per cent because that was a soft subject? When my maths exam results came through, I wept. Thirty-eight per cent. Surely that was it. I could see myself back in the secondary modern, getting beaten up by boys who could only grunt and get drunk.

It was pointed out to me that the excessive anxiety I carried in any area of performance, whether giving a speech, writing an article or doing an interview, was essentially, 'Your inner child is still trying to find out what the grade is.' Put that way, it was easy to access the pain. I remembered the washes of shame and the blushing as my exam papers were handed out in subjects I was weak in, with even the teachers (who knew my secret, fee-paying status) looking sorry for me. I saw that stammering twelve-year-old, with his tousled hair, and his black despair masked by a fierce cheeriness, but the pillow at night would be wet with the anguish of it all. What were we doing as a society trying to determine a person's destiny on the basis of intelligence tests that boys were genetically predisposed to do less well in than girls anyway because they tend to be late developers? Oh yes, I could access the pain all right. Like it was yesterday.

Well, the voice, of course, was trying to spare me the disappointment of not continuing in grammar school. 'You're not going to make the grade' hardened into 'You'll never make the grade'. But the intention was to prevent a total crash when the news came through: 'You've failed your review . . . you need to go to the secondary modern now.' If I internalised that voice that I really wasn't smart enough to be a grammar-school boy, then it wouldn't kill me to end up a secondary-modern-school boy. That's protective, right? So the anxiety – out of bounds though it was – was still out to prepare me for catastrophe. Thank you, voice. I get it, but my whole identity does not rest on whether I really wow this audience, or get a prize for this article.

I did get told those words in a very offhand way, 'Oh, apparently you've passed your review.' There was no celebration. No one said anything. I thought I would go into the next year with a lot less fear, and there was a sense in which school became more enjoyable, but somehow the anxiety levels remained. The voice was winning.

Looking back, years later, I wondered what the deeper longing in that voice was. I think it was that I just wanted to belong. I wanted to be a grammar-school boy. Not a paid imposter. So I thought, well what kind thing can I give myself? I gave myself a golf weekend with friends I liked. There was no grade. No one had to go round in fewer than eighty strokes. The emphasis was not on winning a game, but on enjoying a friendship.

I still need to give myself this kiss from time to time, even thirty years later. A strong voice never goes away. It just needs to be put in its place.

Does yours?

Take its power away by giving it a kiss!

9

#3 Ask God to Share the Burden

Ask God to share the burden! Well, of course. Straight from the land of the bleeding obvious. We are Christians: of course we ask God for help. But the sad and rather universal fact is that we don't ask for God's help half enough! The default setting for the Christian life is to try to live it in our own strength. Bizarre. We say we follow God, but we actually prefer to live independently of him.

There's a very good reason for this, which is beautifully put by the German theologian Helmut Thielicke: 'There is only one desire stronger than the desire for God, and that is the desire to be free of him.' Well said. We struggle to ask God for help because our deepest desire as creatures is to live our lives without him. Put another way, the source of all our unhappiness is a failure to accept that we are creatures and not the Creator. A creature cannot function on its own. It needs help – the help of God and the help of others. If we want to flourish, better learn to shout 'Help!' But if you go back to the Garden, when God came walking our first response was, 'Hide!'

It still is.

That it is hard to shout 'Help!' is due to a very good reason that is not only theological in explanation. A helpful, quite Freudian version of developmental psychology can provide a grid to understand this. We have an ego, which is really a kind of governor. It emerges in our early years and starts to make itself known by shouting 'No' a lot of the time. That's important, because the ego is refusing absorption into mothers, fathers and others, and beginning to build a distinct and unique psychic life that becomes us. The term 'ego' here is used to refer to that which replaces itself at the centre. It's how we grow a self in the first place. So far, so good.

But the problem is that the ego blanks out too much in order to create this self. Dedicated as it is to balancing our survival and pleasure, it tends to railroad us into living life in two dimensions instead of four. We have the self, and the world. That's two dimensions. The ego can handle those. But our existence contains two more dimensions – the void and the holy. The void is the threat of nothingness, and has many faces – such as absence, loss, shame, guilt, hatred, loneliness, and even evil. It is the whisper that whatever lives in this world comes in the end to absolutely nothing. We need its wisdom to realise there is more to life than meets the eye, but the ego can't handle it, or handles it the only way it can – by pretending the dimension doesn't exist. Same with the holy, which is the true Presence in the universe that gives us meaning and hope and enables us to be a proper creature in relationship with a Creator.

The only way we can live life in four dimensions rather than two is to stop the power of the ego to say 'No' to the wider experiences of life. That isn't easy.

What's the point of all this? It is to remember that probably the hardest thing we can do as a human being is to cry to the sacred realm for help.

Still, that's not a counsel of despair, because if a voice is appearing to exert so much power and control in a life, it makes us desperate for help. We've come to that domain in life called 'At-the-end-of-my-rope.com'. That's the place — when all other options are exhausted — where we tend to cry to God. Even extreme addictions can in a sense give us this positive benefit, as Gerard May wrote in his incredible little book *Addiction & Grace*: 'To be alive is to be addicted, and to be alive and addicted is to stand in need of grace.' In a situation like this, the defences of the ego can be overcome, and we shout, 'Help me, God.'

So much, so theoretical. What does it look like in practice? I shared before about once flying to South Africa for meetings. They were quite a big deal, and much was expected of yours truly. Maybe it was exhaustion. Maybe it was chronic under-preparation. But the night before I was due to speak I sat on the floor of the hotel room and gazed appalled at my notes. And up came a voice so strong it was easy to name. I called it Disaster Voice. It threw quite a cluster of phrases at me:

'This is going to be an utter disaster.'

'Everyone is going to think it was a complete waste of their time.'

'Your hosts are going to want their money back.'

'This stuff is so bad you may have to stop in the middle and just apologise and leave the stage.'

Disaster Voice was getting into its stride, but I could just about see the damage it was doing. It was a dismissal voice

– nothing I could do would avert disaster, so don't even try. A heavy dark blanket was settling over my soul. A despair that was rendering me joyless and miserable. I was even shutting down physically, dropping my head and shoulders from the weight of it. But I thought, 'This is crazy. It's one thing to have a few nerves – that I can handle – but where is this black despair coming from, this conviction of disaster? Surely from nowhere good!'

I grew angry about it, and began to shout quietly to God, 'Lord, can you not share some of the load here? I'm down here doing this for you, after all. It's ministry.' Of course, another voice just rushed in and said, 'Of course it's ministry, so just put up with this – this is the battle, what are you so surprised about?'

It occurred to me that I might benefit from a bit of Bible reading (yes, I was very slow and weary), but where to read? I didn't know any obvious bits to counter Disaster Voice. So I got the yearly lectionary and read the passage for that day. It was a passage in Zephaniah. My heart sank even more. But then in the middle of the reading a verse came with the force of an uppercut: 'The King . . . will live among you . . . and you will never again fear disaster' (Zephaniah 3:15).

You will never again fear disaster, because the King is among you. When I tell this story, people say, 'Wow, what a strengthening!' But reading the verse didn't strengthen me. It just excited me. I felt God was speaking back, and making an offer. So I got down on my knees and said, 'Lord, I'm not going to get off my knees until you share this load. I want to feel lighter. Take some of this away. I don't ask for you to lift the nervousness – that's useful. But I do ask for you to lift the blackness – that has no place here.'

I cried out for about three hours before the 'lightening' came.

What a difference it made. I can't say revival broke out that weekend in Johannesburg. It was the usual mixture. Some loved it. Some were indifferent. Some didn't care for it. That's OK. In any form of public speaking you have to learn early that you are never everyone's cup of tea. But the darkness had been dispelled. Disaster Voice had been dealt with . . . for now.

Of course, it's still with me, and when it appears, it revives my prayer life like nobody's business. And I'm always left thinking, 'Why does it take this mess to get me really praying?' Also, I didn't defeat this voice purely by asking God to share the burden. I had to use some of the other tactics too. If voices cluster, then we too need a gang to deal with them. A gang of five!

If there is a process to this – and I know in the heat of battle, processes do not come to mind easily – try these steps. These always come after we have done our SNN – *still, notice and name*. And realise the ADD damage the voice might be doing – *absent, dismiss, deflect*. Try this:

1. WRITE DOWN WHAT YOU CAN NO LONGER DO ALONE

You can't go on. Why not? Be as specific as you can about why this has become intolerable. Why has this particular voice become such a burden? Why is it an elephant sitting on your chest?

2. Invite God to share some of the load

Be careful what you are asking God's help for. A lot of the time the voice is there to make us dependent on him, so just asking him to remove it completely may not be a good prayer. As Augustine says, often God lets us go through difficulties so that what may be known to him about ourselves also becomes known to us. The weakness may be good, but in what way do you need help to stop this becoming debilitating, and what will restore joy and flourishing?

3. Name the difficult feelings and state specifically what you want God to take

Go into the pain and the blackness, and feel it, and then that will be a good guide to what it is you are asking God to do. Do you need a new emotion? A new power? A new confidence? A physical intervention, perhaps? The more specific the prayer, the more we know whether it is answered or not.

4. Note how you will know that God has responded

How are you going to know whether God has helped or not? What do you need to keep monitoring to find out? Over what timescale? Staying alert to this is actually a wonderful part of the adventure of prayer. If God hasn't answered this way, then what is he doing? That can lead to some great experience of God, though it might be a dark and frightening path.

Come to think of it, when we ask for God's help, how do we get strengthened? What does it look like (so we can better notice if God has responded or not)? This is a big topic, but let me just offer these two ways as a starter. God strengthens us by (a) reframing our perspective to see life right, and (b) providing a power with which to endure life.

The great novelist Marilynne Robinson was interviewed in the *Paris Review* not so many years ago.[1] She described religion as a

'. . . framing mechanism. It is a language of orientation that presents itself as a series of questions. It talks about the arc of life and the quality of experience in ways that I've found fruitful to think about. Religion has been profoundly effective in enlarging human imagination and expression. It's only very recently that you couldn't see how the high arts are intimately connected to religion.'

I love that idea of strengthening as a reframe of perspective. Take Job. What is his essential complaint? It comes in chapter 3. Can I forgive God for making the world this way? He looks out at creation and he says, 'It's all dark, I can't see the good.' And Job 3 is in total contrast to the first chapter of the Bible. God makes the world, looks at it and says, 'Oh, it's very good.' Job looks at the same world and says, 'No it isn't; it's very bad.'

Which is quite a major issue. From his vantage point as humanity's chief sufferer, he's got a right to ask. Wouldn't you if you had just lost health, wealth and family, and the only relief you can get from suffering is to scratch your boils with a broken piece of pottery?

1 Marilynne Robinson, interviewed by Sarah Fay 'The Art of Fiction No. 198', *Paris Review*, 186 (2008).

So Job puts all this to God. 'What do you say?' he's asking. 'Have I framed this right, because if I haven't, I'd like some help here.'

Three friends come along and, at first, they are wonderful. They sit with him for a week and say nothing. What empathy. But then they get to talking, and they try to help him by playing a little game called 'hunt the sin'. They had a frame. It was plain. If you do right, you get blessed; if you suffer, you deserve it. So their job – as they see it – is to make Job find those sins in himself that have caused all this trouble to break out upon him. They never get the point though – through thirty-eight chapters of arguing back and forth – that Job hasn't actually got sins that have caused all this. Wrong paradigm, friends. Wrong frame. Wrong friends?

This whole dialogue climaxes with a long, tedious speech from a young cove called Elihu. He says he's been keeping quiet out of respect for his elders, but he's fed up with listening to them going round and round and on and on. So he says, 'Right, it's time for me to sort all this out,' and proceeds to make the longest speech of the book, and he says absolutely nothing new. Total gasbag. Job doesn't even bother replying. Neither do the friends.

And that's where the talking cure gets you. Absolutely nowhere. Job just wants a reply from God. And that's the last few chapters of the book. God finally speaks. With questions like:

- What supports the earth's foundations?
- Who kept the sea inside its boundaries as it burst from inside its womb?

- Have you ever commanded the morning to appear, and caused the dawn to rise in the east?
- Have you seen the gates of utter gloom, where the void is?
- Can you walk on the ocean floor?
- Can you fix the lights of the Pleiades?

And so on. At first, it's quite hard to see how all these questions could help Job, unanswerable as they are. But of course, remember Job's original complaint – can I forgive God for making the world this way? God paints such a giant picture of the universe, stretching it out to its fullest extent, and shows such delight in it, that Job has to accept that his complaint is not a question he can answer. God doesn't either, but makes the point that he is the Creator, and Job the creature. Creatures simply cannot know these fuller mysteries of the universe, and Job is happy to embrace his creaturely status.

You might say that God does not give us answers – we couldn't understand them. But he does give us replies – and that shows that he loves us. He talked to the man with the questions, not to the friends with the answers.

So you can see how this works. Job got to the point where he couldn't stand it anymore. His issue was not solved by more dialogue with friends. He needed to hear from God and only God. And in the end, he gets a reframe. 'The universe is bigger than you think, Job, and only I know its patterns. And those patterns do have mercy and meaning at their core – in a way you simply are not equipped to see.'

A reframe. He can see now. And that is so much of the teaching of the Bible. In John's Gospel it's all about how

Jesus simply teaches us to see. The signs seem to dazzle. Through the suffering, you can see better who he is.

Sometimes, like Job, we need the frame extended. At other times we need the frame shrunk, maybe to dial down to invest that moment, or this day, with all the glory God can give us. Christian mystic Frank Laubach used to argue that everything we need to be perfectly happy is available to us in the next sixty seconds. Shrinking the frame to 'now' is so often a highway to a deeper, more meaningful experience of God. Maybe that's what mindfulness is all about – coming to the present moment without wishing it were otherwise. It requires us to detach, or subtract.

Well, if God strengthens us by reframing our perspective to see life right, we also need him to provide a power with which to endure life, especially when we are at the end of our rope. We need power to get through. And often in the Bible, when God sets out to strengthen his people, he engineers a situation where – if he doesn't intervene – they perish. Just this morning the reading for the lectionary was Exodus 14, where Israel gets chased to the edge of the Red Sea by Pharaoh's armies. They are quaking in their boots, and heartily wish they had stayed behind as slaves on the 'better whipped than dead' reasoning. But Moses says, 'Don't be afraid. Just stand still and watch the LORD rescue you today' (Exodus 14:13). God gives Moses his part to play – hold your hand out, and God plays his part – by sweeping the sea into walls. This is so there is to be no doubt who gets the glory. This pattern repeats in Scripture, but the key point to notice is that the Israelites were delivered to endure forty years of wandering. When Christ is strengthened in the garden of Gethsemane, the angel strengthens him to bear the cross. He is not delivered from it.

I have a long relationship in my life with many persecuted Christians, and years ago I was meeting a great Christian leader in Shanghai called Wang Ming Dao. He heard of my desire to write a book about the persecuted, and he held up a shaking finger of warning: 'When you write our story, make sure for every deliverance story you tell, you also tell a hundred endurance stories – that is the proportion that got us through.'

Which reminds me of the story of 'Worthless Wu', a deprecatory nickname that a famous Chinese scholar gave himself. *You're worthless* was his voice, but there was a painful prehistory to it. Though born in China to a wealthy family, he had left to study in America and excelled to join the law faculty of a major university. But when Mao took over in 1949, many Chinese felt it a patriotic duty to come home and offer their skills so the shattered country could be rebuilt. So he brought his wife and young son back to China in the late 1950s. This was bad timing, however, as the country began to suffer food shortages, Christians were regarded as very suspicious, and a few years later Dr Wu was jailed for his bourgeois background and religious leanings.

Being sent to work in a labour camp was not called 'prison' but 're-education through labour', and although the labour was backbreaking, it was the re-education that was toughest to endure. Every week he was called in to a 'struggle meeting', at which he was expected to recant his religious views and embrace Maoist thought. He was placed on a dais in front of a few hundred people in the crammed hall, and subjected to people interrogating him, shouting at him, confusing him, even beating him on occasions, in the confident belief that he would soon change his mind and join Mao's great social experiment.

He soon realised that he would not survive the experience. Soon he began to shake, and flush with embarrassment. With the hunger, he lost his ability to reason well, and in desperation he cried to the Lord, 'If you don't show me a way to stay strong, I will be broken, and I will fail you.' They shouted at him, 'You are worthless if you don't believe in Mao thought.' He began to feel worthless in his heart.

One day in the fields, as he was weeding a crop, he turned over two small stones, one rough, the other smooth. As he looked up to heaven he remembered the story of a rabbi who taught his followers to place two stones, one in the palm of each hand. On the rough stone was carved the words, *I am but dust and ashes.* On the other, smooth, one was carved, *I am a child of God.*

Dr Wu took the stones, and amended the messages. The rough stone was, *I am but dust and ashes*, and he resolved, 'When I am in the struggle meetings, and they are calling me worthless, stupid and foolish, I will grip the stone and admit, "Yes, they are right, a lot of me is broken. I am prideful, stubborn and stupid. It's true. This is part of me."' But as he gripped the smooth stone, he would say to himself, 'I am a child beloved of God for all eternity.' Despite being made of clay, there was also a sliver of eternity in his being, and his dignity came from the eternal fact that Christ loved him and valued his life so much he came and died for him. Dr Wu said to God, 'You have to get me through. This is all I can do. When I squeeze the stones, I'm praying to you, I'm begging for your help.'

From then on, during the struggle meetings he would grip the stones tightly. Few guessed his secret, but never again did he break down, never again was he tempted to apostatise, never again did he want to give up the faith completely. It wasn't easy, of course, and he did serve the best part of ten years in the labour camp, losing his health from the back-breaking and dangerous work.

But he received the power to endure. He got through with his faith intact. As he squeezed those stones he was asking God, 'Help me, help me, help me survive this struggle meeting, otherwise I will internalise this worthless voice, and I will apostatise in order to have an easier life.' He would not talk much about it but just said tersely, 'God helped. I got through.' The worthless voice was repelled.

There is a poignant postscript to this story. Dr Wu was rehabilitated somewhat after the death of Mao and put in charge of drafting certain laws in a legal department. He would take his two stones and place them on his desk as he read through the proposed legislation. He would touch the rough stone and examine the law asking, 'Does this law reflect that we are fallen creatures? If it assumes we are all perfect, the law will not work.' There must be a realism about human nature since we are but dust and ashes. Then he would grip the smooth stone and read through the law again, asking, 'Does this law reflect and protect the sacred dignity of human beings?' We are special because we are children of God, beloved by Christ. So he brought a realism and ambition the areas of law-making for which he was responsible, even though his

Christian faith was muted and his witness indirect in the law-drafting department of the Chinese Communist Party.

Once a friend visited his department in order to say hello, but he was crushed to hear that Dr Wu had suddenly died, probably worn out prematurely from the years spent down the mines in the labour camp. As he walked away, however, he stopped and rubbed his eyes. On the desks of at least three younger workers, there were two stones – one rough, one smooth. Dr Wu was not worthless. He had passed on his method. He was having an influence even after his death.

See what God did. He got him through. In those struggle meetings, he received the power to endure, otherwise the voices of his accusers would have prevailed. So 'Worthless Wu', as he was nicknamed, refused to receive his identity from this story. Not worthless, but in the power of God eternally loved and eternally useful.

Even today in China some lawyer is drafting a law with two stones on his desk. Because Dr Wu held them tightly in his hands nearly sixty years ago God helped him through, and 'Worthless Wu' became 'Priceless Wu'.

Same God. Same transformation on offer . . . should you choose to cry 'Help!'

10

#4 Shrink the Voice

THE FOURTH STRATAGEM for dealing with a voice is to shrink it. I used to say 'relativise' the voice, but that's a rather ugly, even if accurate, word. The point here is to fill our lives with people and activities that give us so much meaning and joy that even if the voice does its worst in one area, its effects are massively minimised or *boundaried* from other areas. It may steal our joy in, for example, our work, but it cannot in our marriages, or our free time, or our time with God. It is just harnessing the power of a full life. Voices thrive in a vacuum, and a thin life – especially a lonely life – is an easy target. However, as we keep stressing, if you know you are vulnerable to this, then it's a great pointer to the fact that you need to really *live* again!

This dawned on me as a hospital chaplain. I was in the US taking a Masters of Divinity, and part of the programme was to complete a semester as a hospital chaplain. Being a little older than the norm, I was assigned the oncology ward, the Intensive Care Unit, and the Critical Care Unit. So I saw a lot of dying. At the outset, I said to myself (without blushing, I confess), 'I'm sure that Christians die the best. After all, it doesn't end for them. They've got a more undiluted Jesus waiting, and eternal life without tears.' But I have to say that after watching upwards of fifty people die in the time I was chaplain, this conviction was shaken by the facts. Sure, I saw Christians die well, but others died in agony, searching for some sin that had condemned them to miss their healing, or in dread at the impending judgements of the afterlife. Sure, some atheists raged against the dying of the light like Dylan Thomas, but many also slid away in total serenity. I searched for a new if unscientific common denominator, and ended up convicted that it was this: The people who died the best were those who felt they had really lived!

And they had not necessarily filled their lives with great adventures. Often it was just the facts of having raised good kids, or enjoyed a happy marriage, or having grateful people around, or beautiful memories. Remember, I'm not laying claim to revealing any startling truths here. This is relatively obvious stuff – it's just hard to keep it in mind when voices batter us and, as I never tire of saying, a voice is only a voice when you *still, notice and name*. Most of the time it just hits you as a feeling. It's when you stop and say, 'Why am I feeling this anxious?' that the voice becomes clear. Oh, it's the voice that is saying, 'Who are you kidding?' Or the voice that is saying, 'I'm mad . . . I've got to get even.'

It figures, if we remember that voices are about *identity wars*. Most voices want to give us a false and often single identity, and then all our energy gets absorbed by it. But the identity the voice proposes is not worthy of all this energy, and even if we do succeed in satisfying this voice we still won't actually be satisfied in ourselves. It's not rocket science. In fact, in the psychology of wellbeing there is a famous study that says that six elements in life correlate to a feeling of wellbeing. Few have them all, but having even one or two seems to make a massive difference. They are so obvious you could almost guess them: high in social interaction; loves parenthood; enjoys a stable marriage; is involved in some kind of religious practice; has enough income to cover survival needs; spends time with happy people. Obviously not everyone can have all six. Some of us have not had any children, and some have not been fortunate enough to find a mate to marry or, if we have, failed to have a marriage that worked. But still, the idea is that a person who is surrounded by friends and not troubled by survival will probably have a high likelihood of describing themselves as relatively happy. In an even more famous study of high-achievers over fifty years, George Valliant distilled it down to just two factors in the end – a capacity to forgive (including to forgive oneself), and a commitment to maintaining a widening social radius; that is to keep making friends even when your loved ones are dying. It is interesting that, as we get older, our identity is tied less to professional success.

If all you live for is your professional work, then a disaster in that area brings you right down, because there is no resilience residing in the other areas of life. I knew of a man who was a prominent academic. He actually hated his work because his absolute desire was to write a magnum opus on a particular period of history. He had a family but neglected them – they came a very distant second to the production of this world-shattering book. He had friends but they were superficial –

intimate ones could have been too distracting. He had a mother; his father had died and he had struggled even to make it to the funeral, and was appalled to discover he was expected to deliver the eulogy, which he did with a halting grace that failed to hide the fact that he never really knew his father at all. So was the magnum opus progressing? Was he seizing his destiny to write the definitive work in this field? Well, no. The problem was, he was brilliant at administration and was pressured into becoming Dean of Studies, and his life for thirty years was filled with receptions, committees, paperwork, interviews, hiring and firing of staff, a teaching load, and organising everyone else's teaching load. The older he got the more annoyed he became about these dreadful distractions from his life's work, which lay waiting for him. Finally, he snapped, resigned as Dean and negotiated something unheard of in the history of the faculty – a two-year sabbatical at the age of fifty-eight. He hired a cottage on the Canadian coast, loaded up his car with boxes of papers and books, and set off. However, on the journey there he was involved in a dreadful car accident. He lost a leg, was nine months in rehabilitation, and the whiplash from the accident caused such severe head-aches he could only work one day in four. He fell into a deep depression because he had to face the fact that his magnum opus would probably now never get written. This devastated him because he had nothing in his life he could bring to this reversal to mitigate its power. To his credit, he saw that his voice of identity – 'I am destined to write the definitive book on my subject' – had overshadowed and chased away every-thing meaningful from his life. He was able to reconnect with his wife and family through his new, weakened condition, which made him much more compassionate and open as a person. Soon, he began volunteering at a local L'Arche community, where disabled people live together, and was astonished at the rush of wellbeing he received from giving to others without any expectation of return.

He reminded me a little of the character of Casaubon in George Eliot's classic tale of English society, *Middlemarch*. Casaubon was a dyspeptic clergyman of private means who lived for one thing only . . . to produce a key to all religions. Very noble. Very commendable. Very useful. He had filled scores of notebooks with his observations. All that remained was for him to synthesise the learning, write it and publish. His project sounded exciting, and enticed the young, sheltered Dorothea – who was looking for a man of substance – to marry him. But Dorothea quickly found out that he was a joyless man riven by self-doubt and so fixated on this project he was scared to start it. Or, as George Eliot characterises him less prosaically, 'He was a great bladder for dried peas to rattle in.' He would rather just keep amassing notebooks. His fear of revealing his argument to public scrutiny was absolute. When his health begins to break he gets on with it, and Dorothea is never really allowed to become a wife – just a slave to his notebooks. It turns out worse for Casaubon though. He dies without any completion of his project. Dorothea feels she owes it to him to keep going, but soon finds out that his views are derivative and outdated. Casaubon – let the name ring out as a warning – a man of fear who ended up doing nothing but making people unhappy, including himself.

Did I ever mention that voices can be very profound in their effects? So what we are talking about here is, in a sense, any voice that wants to shrink your life down to one thing, so that you lose the ability to flourish in other areas.

Of course, the voice may not be asking us to do something wrong at all. In fact, we often get obsessive about doing the right thing, or even a great thing. Your voice might be saying, 'I have to give my child everything for success,' but if that takes over and you live through the child, the voice has made you overbalance and you are giving it too much power by being unable to balance it out. It is often a positive voice here, such as, 'I must help my country', or, 'I have to save the planet by stopping pesticides'. Even in the Church this can be an issue. I remember a person who was a gifted evangelist. She would tell you, 'I live to see souls saved.' She was dedicated all right. She had shunned marriage, refused to buy a house and lived a life of itineracy, preaching the gospel around China. But in the end it was a rollercoaster that exhausted her to the point of burn-out. She said, 'When I preached, and maybe five or ten would be saved, I would be on cloud nine; but if I preached, and only one or two came forward to offer their lives to God, I would be crushed. It was as if I had failed God as an evangelist.' That's just a voice that needs to be shrunk. She needed more in her life so that the ordinary failure that went with the territory would not have such an impact.

I'm fascinated by sportspeople in this respect, because they force us to deal with the question: When is obsessing over increased performance wrong? After all, we are not out to take the achievement out of life, but to take the obsession out of achievement. Of course we continually emphasise the healing power of stillness, and it has to be stillness before

God, because only then do we take in that in the eyes of God we are worth far more than anything we can possibly achieve. Mere mindfulness cannot get near that. Stilling, noting and naming even by itself can create the space to detach from a false identity, and make it gloriously possible to receive our identity rather than earn it. Well, that's one tactic I suppose, or the undergirding tactic that makes all the others work. *But this tactic of making sure our life is full so the power of the voice is shrunk is not seeking detachment from the power of the voice, but to dilute the effect of the voice.* Sportsmen can point the way here. I remember a superb profile, by the former cricketer turned journalist Mike Atherton, of the then England cricket captain, Alastair Cook. Cook was a run machine but, like any sports figure, he had ups and downs, and had gone a long spell without getting any runs. Worse, his captaincy was being heavily criticised as the team were drubbed by the old enemy, Australia. But Cook still held his head high. He was grounded. The failure to get runs and be a winning captain did not define him. Atherton found out why: 'Cook was a gentleman farmer.' As Cook put it in suitably agricultural terms, 'When you've got your hands down a sheep's gullet, your mind is occupied by thoughts other than your grip, stance and back lift, or the opposition's fast bowler . . . it gives balance in my life.'

Balance in my life? Cook refused to accept that his primary identity was to be England cricket captain. But if he had tried to do that by mere psychological detachment, he wouldn't have managed it. It was because he took his farming, and his family, as seriously as his cricket that he did not succumb to a debilitating achievement addiction. That's what we mean by relativising or shrinking the voice.

I watched very little of the last Olympics, I have to say, mainly because I found it so unattractive to see athletes weeping over getting silver or bronze. Sure, they had trained for gold. But no one is *entitled* to gold, and there are a hundred reasons why you may not get it, even if you are the supreme athlete in your field. You might just wake up with diarrhoea on the day of your final. Tough. You have to refuse to be defined by it, but it was sad to see how few had more in their life than just winning. They had a voice, 'I have to win gold or I'm crap – silver won't do.' All the more refreshing, then, to see probably the world's fittest athlete, the four-times winner of the Tour de France, Chris Froome, come home to claim a bronze and be delighted and generous in his praise of the winner and others. Now, he might have thought – as many did – 'I'm the Tour de France winner – only gold will do,' but for all his fitness and prowess he did not feel entitled to the gold medal. The highlight for me was watching his smile as he received a bronze. I'm sure he was disappointed, but it didn't define him. As a family man, he has a lot more to live for and, maybe even more importantly, other people to live for. But he exhibited the true Olympian spirit – that to compete is the honour! What a contrast to the disgraced former winner of six Tours de France, Lance Armstrong, whose obsession for winning led him to cheat on a monumental scale. A documentary lifted the lid on why he was so driven. It turned out that he liked to humiliate people. He didn't just like winning – that one could understand. But actually he liked winning because he wanted to humiliate his fellow riders. That's weird. And look where it got him. Perpetual ignominy. I hope he knows how to put more into his life now.

Well, OK, the chances are that you – like me – are not a world-beating athlete or sportsman, so how do you get practical with this tactic? First thing is, get to know the voice. *Still, notice and name.* Identify a voice. A common one would be what psychologists often call an imposter voice. For example, 'Who are you kidding, trying to do this? You haven't got it. Look at so and so – they are light years ahead of you. Know your place. Stop trying or you'll just make a fool of yourself.'

Once you get a voice, take a look at this table below. We are asking the question, 'What will not change in these areas even if the fear driving the voice comes true? And if you think it will change, do you need to think about adding more "life" in each of the boxes?'

PHYSICAL	SOCIAL
SPIRITUAL	PROFESSIONAL

Think back to Never-Good-Enough Nigel. He realised that he was too invested in the results of his preaching, so that he was devaluing everything and everyone else. So on the physical side, he realised he had to just spend some time treating his body better. Going to a gym wouldn't cut it – he would end up in the spa restaurant having a drink rather than working the equipment. So the only answer was one-to-one Pilates. After five weeks he never looked forward to any appointment more. It was social. He realised he did not have any social relationship outside a church context. So he joined a motorcycle club. His wife was able to join him too. It was hard because they met on Saturdays, when he was usually obsessing about the sermon, but he found the courage to say, 'It's good enough' and the contact and the fun of the activity meant he ceased to brood on it. In fact, he even found his sermons got better because he was meeting new people with different needs and issues, and he realised he had really been preaching to different versions of himself for the past twenty years. Also, he scheduled in (yes, this was America) a time with his son, who was a moody teenager but wanted to learn golf. It taught him patience on a whole new level, and he was staggered when his son began to share his teenage heart. What a world. In the spiritual box he didn't put anything, except to get himself a fifteen-minute egg-timer and 'just watch the sand fall'. It stilled him, and the fact that there was no content to it gave his mind a break, and he found himself being more creative as a result. Finally, in the professional box, he plucked up the courage to go to an AA chapter. He still doesn't believe he's an alcoholic, so he hasn't made the speech. Perhaps he isn't, but the camaraderie of a group where he doesn't have to pretend, and where he is given all the resources he needs to stop drinking, has released a level of energy he didn't believe he had.

Does the voice still land? Is he still tormented that the latest sermon was a dead loss? Does he still wake in the middle of the night dreading that the Church Board are on their way to sack him? From time to time, yes, but it is definitely diluted in its power.

I once heard an ex-SAS soldier talk about this tactic with typical military bluntness. 'Imagine you are a tin bucket,' he said, 'and this voice is an iron ball. You have to catch it in your bucket, but you are on a secret mission. If the ball clatters into your bucket with a crash, the reverberation will give you away and you will be shot. So what you have to do is fill the bucket up with sand. Soft sand. So that when the pellet falls, all we will hear is a quiet plop. Your secret mission will be safe. Your life will be saved.'

Well, that's quite good. If it does it for you. The voice wants to create a reverberation. It wants to create a circus event. It wants you to stay empty so it can make the maximum noise. Fill up the bucket of your life. Talk to yourself. Will your spouse still love you? Will your mother still take your call? Can you still go to the local book club and be accepted? Will your children still like you? Don't let the voice shrink your identity down to performance.

As I say, it's not difficult. The hard thing is always just identifying the voice. That takes stillness, and suddenly this jolt of emotion is slowed down, frame by frame, and an audible tape is detected. And once you hear it, then you have to fill up your life, even if just for the day!

This morning I got up determined to write this chapter, and I was very anxious. I had booked time in a central London hotel to get on with it. 'What's this voice,' I asked? 'Why am I so anxious?' It was my old friend Imposter Voice. 'Who are you kidding? You can't do this . . . you're not a psychologist etc. etc.' But there was a sense in which I could respond to this by relativising its effect even within the day itself. Yes, I had to have a five-hour writing core, but in addition I wrote myself a list:

- Take a walk.
- Meet a friend.
- See a film.
- Sit in a church nearby and practise Trinitarian gratefulness the Gleb Yakunin way.

Yes, the last one needs a bit of explanation, though you get the general idea from the list that I'm packing my day with enjoyable and meaningful stuff ranging from what engages the body to what feeds the soul. Everyone should practise Gleb's three showers of thankfulness – talk about filling your life bucket with sand!

'A priest loves nothing better than a prophet to stone,' a famous Anglican dean once muttered. Yakunin was a Russian Orthodox priest who was also a prophet, and the top priests of his church lined up to stone him even more than the KGB. In this man's life there lies so much of modern Russian history, and what is all right and all wrong with a historic church that gets too close to the state.

His great sin was to publicly accuse his own church of kowtowing to an atheistic state. He became a parish priest in the Russian Orthodox Church in 1962, but in 1965 – when Westerners were proclaiming free love – he proclaimed that it was time for the patriarch Alexi to jettison links with a state doing its utmost to persecute Christians. His criticism was not well received. He was defrocked. That didn't deter him. He founded the influential Christian Committee for the Defence of the Rights of Believers in 1976, and published hundreds of articles about the suppression of religious liberty in the USSR. That's what got him jailed for five years in one of the most notorious prisons in the gulag. Few emerged from the KGB Lefortovo prison. To top it all, he was sentenced on the evidence particularly of two priests who went into the dock accusing him of 'anti-patriotic activity'. At his sentencing he said, 'I thank God for the destiny I have been given.'

I met him in Manila in 1989, and noticed he was fingering his prayer rope as we talked. He showed me that there were thirty-three beads (one for each year of the life of Christ) and they were divided into three sections of eleven each. 'What saved me in jail,' he said, 'was using those beads to stimulate a morning ritual of thankfulness. Otherwise my voices would have destroyed me.'

Yakunin believed that each morning we must deliberately set ourselves to be thankful to God, as this is the most profound reason we were made by him in the first place. He said, 'You can only thrive under persecution if your attitude is like the Psalmist in 116:12, "How can I repay the LORD for all his goodness to me?"' He said that we become sinful when we have lost our centre of gratitude to God, just as in Romans 1 all the problems come because 'they knew God, but they wouldn't worship him as God or even give him thanks' (verse 21). I forget what he exactly did, but I love the ritual of it, and I try to start each day with the three showers of thankfulness.

1. Speak out eleven reasons why I am glad to be alive in God's beautiful world this day.

2. Speak out eleven more reasons why Christ is such a wonderful Saviour and Lord.

3. Speak out eleven things I must place into the hands of God and let the Holy Spirit work them out.

It's a lovely rhythm. A saving rhythm. And for Yakunin it involves the Trinity. You look up to the Father, from whom all things come, and you are glad; you look at Christ, from whom comes your power. This is how you can be sure God is on your side and will help. Then you give over to the Holy Spirit what you need for that day, accepting that you are not in control of life – God is. Yakunin said, 'It's not easy to be thankful in the gulag, but I was enabled to be, and so my life was not determined by the voices that surrounded me – "you are scum, you are an enemy, you think God will help you but you are in our power" – but by a core of thankfulness that took me to my deepest identity in God the Father, Son and Holy Spirit.'

That's not just the way to thrive in prison.

It's the way to thrive in life.

'But why beads?' I asked him.

'It's not the beads,' he admitted. 'But you mustn't forget we're in a body . . . and the body must be reminded that all our troubles come – to humankind and to society – if we forget God.'

It's just a way of grounding. A way of relativising and shrinking the power of a dangerous voice. Don't knock it. It got a man through five years in the gulag. He came out to become a member of the Russian parliament, drafted a religious freedom law, got to examine the KGB archives, exposed the top leadership of the Russian Orthodox Church as KGB plants, and was excommunicated all over again.

But his witness was worth that of a hundred patriarchs.

Gleb knew how to shrink the voices.

Hear that voice?

Maybe it's time to take an invitation to live from a deeper identity.

Fill your life up.

And let thankfulness overflow into all of life.

11

#5 Create a Community of Contradiction

AGAIN, IT'S SIMPLE but hard. The skill lies not in the profundity of the insight, but in the embedding of the practice. A final way to combat the power of voices that are leading us astray is to create a community of contradiction: a group of others – people you may know, or don't know personally – who act as a group that will cheerlead for you, and send you messages, acting as a counterweight to your controlling voices. Oyez! Oyez! Now hear this: *You cannot defeat a voice alone*! We cannot defeat a voice alone for the simple reason that we are not made to be creatures that flourish alone. We are beings designed for relationship, with God and with others. As the theologians say, we are relational beings because ultimately we are made in the image of a relational God, three persons in harmony, which is hard-stamped onto all of nature. At the risk of over-quoting Father Gleb Yakunin, 'The deepest essence of our life reflects that God is a fellowship of persons.'

Simple but hard, because if we stick with the theological strain (don't worry, not for much longer), we are similarly hardwired to try life independent of God, and therefore also of others. We hate to ask for help; we have an ego inside us that has done good work in order to form our personality, but that over-reaches itself to remain in autonomous control at the price of pushing away any other force that makes our wellbeing dependent on another. And let's face it, in Western societies at least – and increasingly in other ones too, like China – we are pushed towards towering feats of self-reliance and streamed into jobs that isolate us. Individualism started out as a great idea, but if it keeps us alone, it's out of control. In Britain, half of all households are listed as single occupancy. I was attending a mindfulness class of thirty people recently, and we were asked to map our typical day in hour-long chunks. Even though this was a very mixed group, from sad strugglers (that was me) to masters of the universe (definitely not me), we all ended up reporting virtually the same daily pattern: up at seven, off to work, knocked ourselves out until about six, commuted back, rushed dinner, fell into bed shattered at about ten. The only time free was roughly from eight till ten in the evening, but most people were too weary to add anything new into that slot, and if you had kids, even that slot wasn't a possibility. If people gathered to meet friends at all it was once a week at the weekend, and most reported that it was activity-based – like attending church, or playing football – where you didn't get a chance to talk to people in any depth. Where's the scope? Where's the capacity to create a community of contradiction to come from? It isn't easy in the modern world, at least until automation takes off and does a big chunk of our paid work for us.

We need other people alongside us to contradict our voices so we need to be intentional about creating this community. By default we often end up in communities of conformity or confirmation. And we have to beware of assuming that our families and churches are helpful communities of contradiction. They may be, but often they are the opposite. And remember, in the end the best community of contradiction is God himself, and he never stops that ministry.

Grasp all that? Relax. That was the outline of the rest of this chapter. Let's get a sense of what this community of contradiction looks like in action with two stories. Though a real person, let's fictionalise her to 'Fantasy Fiona'. Fiona wanted to be beautiful, but she wasn't. The humiliations of not being asked out by boys at school, and worse – being mocked for her mousey looks by other girls – had made this painfully clear. But instead of facing up to this, she gave in to a fantasy voice, 'I am beautiful and I'm going to pretend to be someone else.' So she sat around at home a lot. Through music and videos, she over-identified with every beautiful female heroine. As she ate and drank more than she should, she wasn't overweight Fiona with the acne on her cheeks at all, but Emma Watson for a couple of hours, or Jennifer Lawrence, or Linda Carter in *Wonder Woman*; as she kept watching the old series so often she could have recalled all the dialogue from memory. Of course, the problem with a strong fantasy voice like this is that it makes the real world a very unattractive place.

She did have a set of friends. School rejects like her. They met for drinks twice a week and got drunk. They all let themselves go. They did not form a community of contradiction – more a community of confirmation: You are right to let yourself get overweight, get drunk. And while we are on it, aren't men just awful?

However, one day she was encouraged to do the exercise *still, notice and name*. Her fantasy voice came up and she suddenly grew scared of the power it was exerting. She set out intentionally to find people who would change her self-image and keep her in the world of reality. She volunteered to work with disabled children at the weekends, giving up an entire Saturday to feeding little people with shrunken bodies and mental health barriers. Yet, as she did – and this took a long time – she began to blossom in their absolute love for her. She could pick up on a grunt, or an excited shake of a head, that told her she was beautiful to them. As Jean Vanier says, disabled people have no defences, so their fragility is what you end up loving, and that heals you too as you embrace your own fragility and weakness. She changed churches, to one with a home group that was a great mixture of people, all trying, not many of them attractive, and super-accepting. She also saw her old friends a lot less.

That was all. Just a couple of places where she suddenly found herself valued for who she was, not for who she wished to be. Doesn't look like much? Well, she had successfully created a community of contradiction. It wasn't large. It doesn't need to be. The voice receded, and she could accept who she was and return to the real world as a place of adventure.

Another person with a very different voice. Let's call him 'Vengeful Vince' (OK, OK, even I am starting to think this is getting very corny). He was fired from a bank in the aftermath of the 2008 financial meltdown. No particular reason. They just made cuts one day on the trading floor for reasons they kept to themselves. Five minutes later he was walking out of the door with a box of papers and knick-knacks. Oh, and a furious attitude that began to darken his whole life. He was justly angry at his sacking, the more so as he knew that some of his trading friends had been retained because of a certain compromising scheme they were part of that also implicated the HR supervisor. He had refused to join on ethical grounds, and the thanks he got was being fired first. His voice, though – when he thought about it – was one of revenge: 'They'll regret it . . . I'm going to kill them for this.'

For the best part of a year he tried to get in at other banks, but no one was hiring. He took a low-paid job as a barista, and it seemed that with every coffee cup his hatred grew. He teamed up with a couple of disgruntled former bank employees and began a vicious, anonymous blog trying to smear the bank that had sacked them. He later said, 'We felt even more angry when we realised we had discovered another variant of "Too big to fail", which was, "Too black to smear".' His world was also small. Just traders, ex-traders and wannabe traders.

One day, though, he couldn't put off meeting his sister any longer. He trailed along to lunch with her. What she said brought him to his senses. 'Vince, where are you? You're dead from rage. This thirst for revenge has given you a cold heart.' With tears in her eyes she said, 'Where's my brother gone? Is that kind and caring person still in there?'

He blew her off at the time, but as the weeks flew by he realised she was right. He saw that his voice was one of revenge, and how dangerous it was, but who could he talk to? The only people he knew were all like him. 'Who do I turn to?' he asked himself. Then he thought, 'How about Alexandre Dumas, the author of *The Count of Monte Cristo*?' Like the Count, Vince had been wronged. Like the Count, he was consumed with plotting revenge on those who had brought him down. But how did the story end? He read the story again and again, because it told him with the jolting power that only great storytelling can deliver – a life dedicated to revenge will make you miserable . . . even if you gain justice in the end!

A dead writer had joined his community of contradiction. He also arranged to visit his sister more often, and her cheer-leading brought him back to who he really wanted to be. Moral? A community of contradiction can also include the dead!

Which leads us to attempt a list of what a community of contradiction might consist of beyond the obvious one of finding a circle of people:

- *It does not have to be large.* Sometimes two different people can be enough, though obviously the more the better.

- *It doesn't have to always involve the living.* Vince used Alexandre Dumas. I don't know where I would be without St Augustine, Helmut Thielicke, Bach, Rembrandt and Oscar Wilde. It's all about the strength of the voice involved. If their voice carries a lot of weight, build them into your community of contradiction.

Something might happen to someone in the liturgy, for example. An evangelical I met at seminary found the Orthodox liturgy was so affirming of significance in all ages of time and beyond, and he was struggling with an insignificance voice. So the sheer eternal dimension of the liturgy came to him 'like a deep warm bath'.

- *It can be an atmosphere that is absorbed.* Some locations or groups carry an implicit set of values that just seep in and contradict the voice in question.

- *It can involve the careful curing of memories.*

This last one is interesting. I have a very inspiring friend, but as a child her father had abused her terribly. Though a famous scientist in the academy, he was a monster in the home. The family was quite religious, and one of the messages the father would give her when exasperated was, 'God hates you.' That was when she was four. A defining moment took place when she was five and a half. The family were having a party, and the father noticed that someone had stolen a slice of the birthday cake. It wasn't her, and she denied it when accused, but he was convinced it was. He locked her in a dark cupboard and said, 'Unless you admit you took that slice of cake, you can't come out.' She was in there for twenty-four hours. Like any child seeking to survive, she had to accept that her father was a dangerous man, and she would need to lie to get by. No wonder she developed multiple personality disorder.

Many years later I met her, and knowing what had happened I asked her, 'Did you feel like God abandoned you?' I was astonished frankly that the parental 'God hates you' voice had not developed into some malevolent force. 'Oh no,' she said, 'not after what happened to me at Sunday school.'

She had been taken only once, which makes her story all the more incredible. The teacher gave each child a set of coloured crayons and a stiff piece of white card about seven inches square. 'Now draw the most beautiful house you can imagine,' said the teacher. So my friend drew this wonderful home, and as she was later to be an artist she made an amazing job of it. Then the teacher came around and said, 'Isn't that lovely. Now, I'm going to pin this beautiful house on your chest, and your job is to remember – *this is where God lives.*'

That was all. That was it. As a six-year-old she really took it in. She still remembers the amazement – that God would live in a beautiful house like that *in me*? And so, when her father would say, 'God hates you – he can't love you, you are too terrible,' she would always remember, 'oh yes he does – he lives in the house I drew for him, in me.'

It was her little-big secret. And God's. And it repelled the voice of her father. But through the tough times, she had to re-access it. She always had a drawing of a beautiful house on her fridge, and she was a great believer in compiling a 'compassion board', a cork board on which she pinned drawings and mementoes that sparked her brain to remember that God loved her unconditionally. Her memories became part of her community of contradiction. And here's a wonderful thought . . . *you* could be functioning in someone's community of contradiction without knowing it, even years afterwards, just like that Sunday school teacher, whose name is not even known to my friend.

Is that getting too hard to follow? Or a bit weird? For most Christians, their primary communities tend to be family and church. Can families be cultures of contradiction? Well, yes, of course, but it is a fact that often the toughest voices we struggle with – especially the critical ones – come from our family of origin and it can be very difficult to find alternative voices within it. Families are often the least able to accept that we can change. Parents have ways of keeping a child infantilised, even as an adult. Often, to deal with a voice may require a differentiation from our families, and that seems to be a developmental fact. It's not that most of our families are feral, though some are. It's just that those who know us best or the longest (not necessarily the same thing) have the least expectations of our capacity to change, and often they will discourage us from the desire to change in order not to upset the delicate family dynamics.

Remember Get-Ahead Gerald? He did what a lot of very wealthy westerners do when they try to find themselves – he flew to India to an ashram. Beatles-style. He found a suitable swami, a guru, because he needed to find people who took the spiritual life seriously – if not more so than, the physical life. Such was his desire, he flew half way around the world in order to live differently to his voice, which was 'Get rich – that's all that matters'. But when he comes home, he struggles to find enough friends. And his family just think he's a flake. They do not want to know him, because instead of showing any curiosity about his life, they are fearful that this will change the primary role in which he has been cast and on which they are dependent – that of uninterested super-provider!

Can churches be cultures of contradiction? Again, yes of course, but it has to be said that churches are on the whole places of conformity. We have to behave to belong. But if we develop different views to the prevailing voices, then the church may not be a culture that helps but one that hinders. I was intrigued to read the ruminations of a man who might bear the mantle of conservative Christianity's best known psychologist, Dr Larry Crabb. In a recent book entitled *Real Church: Does It Exist? Can I Find It?* he freely confesses his frustration: 'I am fed up with churches that anchor us in the blessings of the Father, but not in the person of the Father.' He added,

> After talking with thousands of churchgoing people and looking under the surface of their lives to see what is really going on beneath, I don't believe (with few exceptions) that the church in America is doing what God most wants done in the depths of people's lives. We're not penetrating the denial that keeps our worst sins and most terrifying fears out of sight. And worse, I'm not at all sure that we have a clear vision of what God wants to do in our lives. It's difficult to aim your arrow toward a bull's-eye you don't see. (p.20)

For Larry Crabb, the Church failed to be a place that nurtures. 'The difficult truth is that I am profoundly *not* okay, and neither are you . . . I want to be part of a church that knows two things clearly: (1) that I'm a mess, and (2) that God is love' (pp.59–60). Crabb is so refreshing in his honesty about his struggles to find a church where both are affirmed.

I think his point is well made. The Church does not treat broken people that well. They tend to be bracketed out as problem projects. As that famous T-shirt had it, *blessed are the cracked, for they let in the light*. Where's that gone? It's probably not wrong, but the Church needs to be run by upstanding, well-heeled citizens who keep their problems – if they have them – nice and discreet. It's that group that keeps the building up, the programmes running, the pastor and co-workers paid. If you are coming apart at the seams, church may not be for you.

That said, I like to say that *three* churches are part of my community of contradiction, especially of that voice – so prominent in today's materialistic Western society – that *religion is just a total irrelevance that usually does more harm than good*. I need to access the drama of three churches: *Church Magnificent; Church Triumphant; and Church Mediocre*.

The drama of Church Magnificent. That's Bach. That's Handel. That's St Augustine. That's Galileo. That's Rembrandt and Van Gogh and Kandinsky. That's Tolstoy and Dostoyevsky. Great creators who gave us the ideas and arts to show us what an incredible world we live in, what an amazing God we have, and what a privilege it is to be alive. Say what you like, they did it all out of love for God, and in the power of God.

The drama of Church Triumphant. For me, this is the story of the persecuted church. Where Christians overcome incredible odds of suffering and through the blood of their testimony show me that God is a presence that is real even in the midst of excruciating pain, never thwarted in his will, not even when evil does its worst. I need their story when my world goes dark from time to time, to keep believing that God can still work it all out for the best (Romans 8:28).

But the drama of Church Mediocre – what is that? Usually the local church. One church I went to not so long ago felt like taking God's funeral every Sunday. And on the surface, it was so utterly unattractive you would not want to join it. It was a bunch of wilted saints falling out over trivial slights and daft ideas. I remember one exhausting spat over whether attendance figures were correctly recorded, and if giving should continue to a certain aid agency that no longer employed only Christians in developing countries. It would be easy to miss the real drama. But lift the lid on these lives that bitch and bicker, and peer in, and you will find a quiet but compelling drama of how they find God enough to get through. Despite all the silliness, there is underneath a belief in the goodness of God that is experienced, and their story keeps me going. Christianity works . . . though often not in ways we expect, and it's these overlooked lives, that seem devoid of drama on the face of it, who have walk-on parts in an ongoing spiritual drama called *Just Coping* that can carry me too . . . if I pay the price to notice. George Eliot's novel *Middlemarch* ends with this epitaph about the central character, Dorothea:

Her full nature . . . spent itself in channels which had no great name on the earth. But the effect of her being on those around her was incalculably diffusive: for the growing good of the world is partly dependent on unhistoric acts; and that things are not so ill with you and me as they might have been, is half owing to the number who lived faithfully a hidden life, and rest in unvisited tombs.

Three cheers for Church Mediocre. If we really see the lives who commit 'unhistoric acts' and will rest or are resting in 'unvisited tombs' and how they came through to make a difference with the help of God, this can get us all to the 'far side of the river' as the spirituals have it.

Mind you, in itself Church Mediocre would not be enough. I need all three. But the combined power to contradict Danger Voice is mind-blowing. Maybe even more usefully, they show how this community can reveal the Divine Voice that re-centres us – the goal of all we are striving for in this earthly game of identity wars.

Allow me to introduce you to one of my community's characters from Church Triumphant. His real name can never be revealed, as he is what is known as a BMB – a believer from a Muslim background. In the Middle East especially, to be a BMB is to experience ostracism from one's family of origin, and often extreme violence from a Muslim state that will not acknowledge anyone's right to secede from Islam.

This man – call him Abdul – was a jihadist. Very committed. Very extreme. He was taught that to rape a Christian woman was an act of virtue. He came to the Christian faith in a dream, and that's when his problems began. He went along to a church, but instead of welcoming him, they reported him to the authorities, fearful of displeasing the government and inviting persecution by helping a BMB.

He was put into jail. Strung up by his thumbs. An electric cattle prod was shoved into his orifices. Still, he would not recant.

'OK,' said his jailers, 'it's time for you to have *the experience.*'

'What's the experience?' he managed to gasp.

'We put you in a five-foot-square stone box. No light. And leave you there for a month, with just a bit of water and food pushed through every day.'

Abdul's first thought was, 'What's so wrong with that? At least I'll be away from the torture.' And he said to himself, 'Well, I'll just keep praying to Jesus – that will get me through.' He looked at the faces of his jailers and realised he had spoken his thought out loud.

They looked at him, puzzled. 'Everyone goes insane in that box.'

'Why?'

They answered as if to an idiot child: 'Because of the voices. The voices will get you.'

'What voices?'

'Your voices!'

So in he went to the stone box that constituted *the experience.* No one had come out sane.

He sat there in the pitch black. And as the time went by, sitting in his own excrement, sure enough up came the voices.

It was as if every awful thing he had ever done was projected onto a vivid screen on the wall of the cell. And the more he looked, the more he saw how terrible he was.

He said later, 'Normally we are able to hide ourselves from what we are really like, because the ego is well defended. But pain and suffering change all that, because all the weak points of your personality come up to the surface and you can't defend against them. You are too weak to mount the usual defences. When the defences are down, the voices charge in. Voices of condemnation: You're rubbish. You don't love God. You're so full of pride. How could you have done that terrible act to your sister?'

After a couple of weeks he was reduced to a weeping wreck. 'I was crying all the time, till I thought I would fill up the cell with my tears and drown in them. I came face to face with how awful I really was. I kept seeing myself in the crowd where Jesus was paraded by Pilate, and shouting *Crucify him, Crucify him*. And I thought, is that me? Yes it is. I'm there. Looking at him bleeding and shivering, and I'm still shouting, *Crucify him.*'

Just when he was about to collapse into complete despair, and probably into insanity, suddenly he heard a voice like a stream of bubbling water.

It said, '*I still love you . . . as you are!*'

Adbul said, 'It was like a star exploded in that space. Hundreds of points of light in the dark, spinning and twinkling like diamonds against a black velvet cloth.

Jesus loves me . . . as I am.

'Me. Sitting here in my own filth, knowing how awful I am, and still he loves me?' Then he added this amazing line, 'Christ rushed in and filled me, and the filling was so great, because I was so empty.'

That is the great untold secret of the persecuted Church. They are *stilled* to *notice* and *name* in the midst of great privation and pain, but as the condemnation voices crescendo, of accusation, condemnation, futility, this Divine Voice drowns them out: 'I love you as you are.'

When they dragged him out after a month, stinking though he was, they could tell immediately they were witness to the first prisoner who had survived *the experience*.

Persecution is an extreme form of suffering, and in general serves to empty us, making us ready to be filled by God.

But this is one of the wonderful truths of what we are discovering. This is at the heart of what the Divine Voice does. As our voices confront us, and we sense how weak and hopeless and pathetic we are, and just as they seem to peak and define who we are, up bubbles this Divine Voice that says, 'Ah, wait, that's not you. This is you – beloved by God. I love who you really are.'

And if you have been emptied out by those voices, the filling from this voice is all the greater.

Try to bask a little in this voice now. Read these words from Isaiah 43 very slowly. This is the Divine Voice that comes from that deepest place to speak to us in our emptiness.

> *Do not be afraid.*
> *I am the one who formed you.*
> *I have ransomed you.*
> *I have called you by name.*
> *You are mine.*
> *When you go through deep waters, I will be with you.*
> *When you go through rivers of difficulty, you will not*
>   *drown.*

When you walk through the fire of oppression, you will not
   be burned up.
The flames will not consume you, for I am the LORD, *your*
   God, the Holy One of Israel, your Saviour.

Did that help? Depends how empty we feel of course, but
if our voices have served to empty us, the filling is all the
more joyful. I could not do without the drama of the
Church Triumphant, which gives a very different twist to
what we normally mean by triumph, just as the disciples
in the upper room stumble, trying to comprehend how
Jesus could talk about being tortured to death in terms of
being 'glorified'. New rules for drama when it comes to
the Bible.

A quick reminder as to what steps we might take to build
our community of contradiction. *Still, notice, name.* Then,

- *Identify one voice.* Think of people who have said things
  that contradict that voice. They might be living or
  departed, friends, families, teachers, colleagues.
  Conscript them.

- *Think of one thing you can do to build your community of
  contradiction.* This usually involves a ferocious fight to
  make room in a busy life, and the busy lives of others.

- *Think of a person in your life for whom you can be part of
  their community of contradiction.* As we have seen, this
  works both ways. Maybe one of the most lasting acts we

can do is to be a cheerleader for someone, even if it's not on a regular basis.

- *Don't forget God is part of your community of contradiction.* Access his voice. It's always there, but he does tend to whisper.

Of course, the wrong community of contradiction can be a very dangerous thing – which partly reveals the power of the tactic. A lot of literature in the field of de-radicalisation shows that Muslim terrorists are often recruited by a tactic known as 'love bombing'. A lonely, alienated individual is targeted, and then surrounded by a group that gives them the love and acceptance they have never received before. So overwhelmed are they by the experience that they will do anything to stay in the group, even when asked to commit an atrocity to maintain their membership.

Let's not forget, too, that societies or subcultures have powerful voices that we need to get into communities to contradict, but they can be harder to hear because they are quite diffused. I was hearing of a group of Christian scientists who get together secretly on an American campus where they teach. They are secret because there is a dominant voice on the university faculty that religion is for stupid people. It is a sad fact that if their Christian faith is made too explicit, they will be tarred unfairly as 'Bible-bashing fundies', even though ironically this voice can itself best be termed as atheistic funda-mentalism. But it's that form of fundamentalism that garners the research funds. Still, they needed to meet to assure them-selves that they are not stupid. Someone once said, 'If everyone tells you that you are a donkey, eventually you will start looking for your tail.' They are getting together to stop looking for their tail. Cultures contain lies, and you may need an alternative community to stop that lie seeping in.

Maybe this is what has happened, at its most profound level, with the Alpha courses. When I first came across them as a Christian I thought, 'How's that going to work? The content is unremarkable, the teaching merely adequate to good, and will people ever commit to a ten-week meeting plan?' But three million people in Britain alone have gone through an Alpha course of some description, and I'm convinced that the secret lies in its community of contradiction aspect. Most people in the UK now, who are not Christians, rarely know anyone who is a Christian, let alone any of the tenets of the Christian faith itself. But when they finally attend a course, and get to meet Christians and form a community over the ten weeks or so, it is this more than anything else that makes them receptive to the truths of Christ. In my Edinburgh church I heard a new convert confess publicly, 'Before I started Alpha, I really thought that Christians were part of the two-headed brigade. I assumed they were miserable aliens. But getting to know them, realising they were actually quite happy, normal, one-headed people, made me receptive at last to the truth.' That's a community of contradiction in action.

Your voices are probably going to gang up on you. They cluster. They mug. Maybe in desperation. Your trump card may be to gang up on them back . . . with your very own created community of contradiction.

It takes a group to beat a group.

12

God and Our Voices

AT THE START of this journey, we said that voices come from three places: God; the pit; and ourselves. In practice, most of our voices come from ourselves, and even the tempter uses our own voices more as he works best from the shadows. But it's time to finally talk a little more about the role of God's voice in particular.

If Never-Good-Enough Nigel is reading this (you know who you are) then you will like the next sentence, which contains a nice three-pointer on God's voice in the Bible. Here it comes. *God's voice creates – take your place; God's voice calls – take your journey; God's voice whispers – take your fullness!* That's for free, Nige.

God's voice creates. That's Genesis 1 of course. Everything in creation comes about as a result of God's word. The refrain throughout the chapter is, 'And God said . . .' And all as the result of the Divine Voice, galaxies burst into being, seas surge up from barren rock, forests claw through the topsoil, men and women stand tall in all their glorious dignity in a pleasure garden hissing with fecundity. All as a result of a word. That's power. Most of us have to speak and then do. God's speech is an act in itself. Sovereign stuff.

This voice continues to preserve creation. It's ongoing. Remember the disciples in the storm on Galilee, and Jesus has the temerity to be asleep on a cushion through it all. They wake him. 'Don't you care if we drown?' they screech at him in their terror, and this must have been quite a storm to have seasoned fishermen this frightened. So he stands up. Voice says, 'Silence, be still,' and the storm subsides into a calm. But here's the kicker: Jesus turns to them and almost expresses surprise or even disappointment: 'Why are you afraid? Do you still have no faith?' (Mark 4:40). After this, the Scriptures say, the disciples were 'absolutely terrified'. 'Who is this man? . . . Even the wind and waves obey him!' Typical of the Scriptures, when the Divine Voice puts in an appearance, the result is usually petrified humanity. But, on a human level, what's so bad about being scared in a storm? Any person who has spent time on the sea in a small boat learns to respect the sea's moods. You live longer if you have fear of a force 8 or more. But in this instance, Jesus has no time for that attitude. Why is he disappointed? It's surely because they did not realise he was divine. Or more specifically, *he's the same Voice that called wind and waves into being*! The whole story harks back to the end of the Flood where, in Genesis 8 the Scripture says, God sent a wind and the waters receded. Poor disciples. Jesus had hoped they would make the connection – the person who spoke the world into being, and who called to the floodwaters to subside, that's the same person who calmed the storm. Only difference . . . he's in a human body.

That explains Jesus' disappointment. They are not understanding who he is. If they were, any storm need not be feared. He stills it. He shows who he is. They don't get it. They don't get him.

They do eventually, though. It's a great story and in the early church this was a favourite passage to illustrate the two natures of Christ. He sleeps because he's tired. That means he's really human. He also sleeps because he's God. Wind and waves can hold no terror for the Creator. And that was a great comfort to those on their way to face their impending storm – to be torn apart by wild animals for the amusement of the proletariat. If the Divine Voice had taken human form – it showed he loved them to become like them, but also it showed he had the power to take them into glory after death. Love and power. This story *always* goes on with Jesus, the Divine Voice.

Like it? So if this Divine Voice is speaking, creating, re-creating and sustaining this world, our response must be simply this: take your place in it! The source of all our unhappiness in the world is the refusal to accept that we are creatures and not the Creator. We'll take our place then . . . as creatures! This world in which we live is not built to human scale, but divine scale. There are things that will always be beyond our comprehension, and outside our sphere of influence. Fine. We're not running the world. God is. And if I look at the kind of political leaders apparently in charge of big important countries around the world today – Putin, Xi Jinping, Erdoğan, Modi – I'm so glad I don't have to put any faith in them. I'll put it in the One who speaks!

That's the first element of Divine Voice. It locates you in the entire universe. Gives you your role, and your song.

The world does not shrink down to you or me. Or your purpose. Or my legacy. I'm bracing myself for when I walk into a bookstore a few years hence and see this book in an old, secondhand-bookshop basement, probably sold cheap as a 'remainder'. Doesn't matter. It's God's world. Not ours. It's in his hands. Not mine. We have been invited to be part of it entirely through generosity on God's part. I've always loved a sermon by Elizabeth Achtemeier. It's called 'God the Music Lover'. She asks the question 'Why did God make the world?' in the light of a comment by Karl Barth, who said, 'The miracle is not that there is a God. The miracle is that there is a world.' God doesn't need our fellowship. So why did God make the world at all? Achtemeier's answer, a little whimsical I admit, is because *God loves music*!

All creation does try to sing a song of praise to its Maker. We think it is just poetic licence and exaggeration when the Psalmist talks about the universe singing and praising God, or when Job speaks of the morning stars singing together . . . I shall never forget a talk Lesslie Newbigin gave once about the nights he spent in the jungles of India. He said the dark was full of sounds – the roar of lions, the shrieks of jackals and the jabbering of monkeys. 'And', asked Newbigin, 'who hears all these things – there in the depths of the jungle of India night after night?' Well, God hears them. His creatures sing him songs in the night, and God loves the music and is very pleased that his creation is very good.[1]

[1] Elizabeth Achtemeier, *Preaching as Theology & Art* (Nashville: Abingdon Press, 1984), p.64.

Termites make percussive sounds in their nests, even producing bell-like notes. Humpback whales sing, and it's not only to find mates. They breach and leap clear of waves, showing the sheer pleasure of jubilation. We're supposed to join this praise. And remember . . . God loves you more than he loves all creation. Sing your song. Take your place.

Second, though, *God's voice calls, 'Take your journey.'* The prologue to the Bible is Genesis 1–11. We get what the creation is for, and where it went wrong, culminating in a lost world, after Babel, that has to scatter to survive. Into this situation God's voice speaks . . . to a man called Abram (Abraham). Doesn't seem like much at first. Nations are struggling in mutual incomprehension. God says, 'don't worry, I'm on it.' Oh, thank goodness. Are you sending an army? A leader? A plague?

'No, I'm calling a man. One man. And by the way, he won't be a nation for at least four hundred years!'

All throughout the Bible, the whole plot of God's action in this world, to deal with what's going wrong, is to call people through his voice. Abraham was the first: 'Leave your native country, your relatives, and your father's family, and go to the land that I will show you. I will make you into a great nation. I will bless you and make you famous, and you will be a blessing to others . . . All the families on earth will be blessed through you' (Genesis 12:1–3).

And so, as Peter Berger (a great sociologist and part of my community of contradiction) says, we have the beginning of individualism. Abraham is called out from his tribe, from his city, from his religion, and told to take another journey, with just three promises in his backpack. I will give you descendants, they will be numerous; I will give you a land for these descendants, they will be a nation; and I will use them to bless and reconcile the whole world. The whole plot line of the Bible is how God overcomes the obstacles to bring all this about. Abraham hasn't got a son. Israel hasn't got a land. The people of Israel don't want to help the world. Isaac, Canaan and Jesus are the answers . . . over a couple of thousand years.

Well, that's the voice of God. It stops key individuals in their tracks, turns them right around, takes them away from their tribal or religious destiny, and makes them serve the will of God in remaking this world. Prophets and kings hear this voice. Samuel as a teenager. Jesus heard it at least twice. Paul hears it famously on the way to Damascus, where he is about to commit religious genocide. Peter hears God's voice saying, 'Kill and eat' in a vision that teaches him to extend the gospel to those beyond the Jewish enclave. The point of a voice like this, though, is that it usually sets us on an unexpected journey, taking a very opposite track or tackling a huge obstacle.

The question is, to what extent should we expect to hear this voice today? Is it unusual? Is it rationed? Is it rare? Certainly it is unusual, even in the Bible. If it was that critical to hear the voice of God in personal address, it would surely have been happening to Jesus in every chapter, and to the apostles every six verses. Maybe we are supposed to view a hearing of the Divine Voice in the same way as we are to treat a supernatural sign – wonderful to receive it, but fatal to clamour for it. Most of us experience the call of God as a claim upon us but not with a voice in a vision. I'm personally uncomfortable with Christians saying airily, 'God told me to . . .' and 'God spoke and gave me this word . . .' It's the language – which misdescribes it – that worries me, rather than the experience. What most of them really mean is that they have a strong impression of divine guidance. They haven't heard a voice or had a vision. It's just rhetorical short-hand for a strong impression, but it creates awkwardness because how can you say back to someone, 'Actually, I don't think that *is* the best way,' when they feel God's just told them it has to be this way? It short-circuits discernment, and refuses to accept that discovering the will of God is best done communally, not individually.

My great hesitation on this, though, comes from my experience of the global Church. We are living in remarkable times, when the Church in Asia and Africa has exploded numerically, and even the Islamic world has seen literally hundreds of thousands of converts turning to Christ in recent decades. This is unprecedented, but according to the best reports I have seen, approximately 50 per cent (that's the lowest credible percentage) of believers from a Muslim background (BMBs) became Christians because they heard the Divine Voice speak to them in a dream, often in a vision of Christ or Mary. It's not the norm, but on the other hand, an experience like this is not far off the norm, for this particular category of new Christian. I was meeting a Saudi Christian, who found Christ while making the *Hajj*. Sleeping in a room full of Muslim pilgrims, Jesus suddenly appeared to him in a dream. 'He was so much bigger than Mohammed,' he said, 'and he said to me – "It's really me you are seeking."' He woke up in a sweat, continued on the *Hajj*, but his heart was no longer in it. On a trip abroad he secretly read a New Testament, and professed Christianity, but he could not run the risk of taking the Scriptures back into Saudi Arabia. 'It's too risky. If the authorities find a Christian Bible on my person, they will interrogate me, and I will not lie, so my new faith would be exposed.' He longs to tell his wives (he has three), but he dare not. Saudi Arabia adheres to a hard-line Islamic fundamentalism called Wahhabism, as do other Gulf States such as Qatar, and Saudi nationals are strictly forbidden to convert away from Islam, on pain of death. 'I do not know how long I can go without fellowship, without witness, living a lie,' said this Saudi Christian. But he is so typical of many BMBs in the world today that I suspect the Divine Voice is experienced quite widely, and perhaps particularly among those for whom coming out of their present life could cost their lives.

At any rate, should you hear the Divine Voice – usually in some kind of dream or mystic experience – get ready to *take your journey*, and *take your stand*. A new path must be trodden, and new lions are in the way.

There is a third strand of teaching, however, about God's voice in the Bible. *God's voice whispers, 'Take your fullness!'* There's a very important but uncomfortable fact in the Bible. We read of all the oracles of prophets and the visions of apostles; we read the clear teachings of Jesus, and Moses lists the miracles of deliverance for the Israelites and says, 'He showed you these things so you would know that the LORD is God and there is no other. He let you hear his voice from heaven so he could instruct you' (Deuteronomy 4:35–36). But the awkward fact is that the people do not hear this voice as unambiguous or as a foghorn, nor are they moved to obedience. Indeed, there seem to be many loudspeakers on the street, and many miracle-makers with alternative messages. Fake news seems to trump truth all through the Bible (no pun intended). For some time, the wizards of Egypt match Moses miracle for miracle. The majority of prophets in the time of Amos and Jeremiah were saying the opposite of those men whose words became Scripture. Even Jesus couldn't get a large crowd to deeply comprehend his message, and matters were not helped by resorting to parables with meanings that were far from clear. He was only figured out in his lifetime by a very few. This is the fact. God speaks, but he whispers. He does not crush through weight of evidence. We are given the invitation to listen and see, and the option to refuse to follow. A foghorn voice, a consuming fire, a pillar of cloud – they happen, but even then they don't seem to command assent. God's voice is in everything, but it does not compel. It needs to be seen. It whispers, rather than shouts, and as Fred Craddock writes, 'The painful truth about the whisper is that not everyone hears it.'

I used to think that the most frustrating truth was this; that God can be so everywhere it looks like he is nowhere! He pervades everything, but you have to learn to see. See God in the stars. See God in the leaf. See God in the ugly face as well as the pretty one. See God in the deliverance but also in the endurance. See God in the parable as well as the miracle. God's voice is there, but it's hushed, hushed to draw us forward and draw us up in all our dignity and to work with him. The question is, though, why is this better than the unequivocal?

Think of it this way. Jesus could have stayed on the earth and sent the Holy Spirit too. It would have brought amazing advantages. We would have the world's only two thousand-year-old man alive and well. We could do scientific tests on his skin, and prove that he is eternal in body. We could fill stadia, and he could heal by the tens of thousands. We could have twenty-four-hour teaching streamed from his mansion in Jerusalem. We could have nations advised with perfect foresight. Nothing is impossible for God. Jesus could have stayed on the earth. But the better idea, he said, was for him to go to heaven and send the Spirit instead. Why? Why is it better for us that 'a cloud hides him from our sight' (cf. Acts 1:9) even today? The answer must lie in the result – it makes us come to him and makes space for our fullness. Jesus does not seek to overwhelm. He seeks to co-operate. If his voice was unambiguous, there would be no choice, no freedom. We would obey out of terror. God has taken a greater risk – to turn his voice into a whisper and give us the space to co-create this world. Big risk. Beautiful faith.

The upshot is that we have to *discern* the voice of God. Yes, it would have been easier if Jesus had just appeared when the early Church was having a high-powered pow-wow about whether Gentiles should be included in the gospel effort, and if so, on what terms? There was a lot at stake in this conference recorded in Acts 15, but Jesus stayed 'behind the cloud'. Paul feared that if these leaders made it too difficult for Gentiles to convert, i.e. they would have to become Jews first, it would stop mission in its tracks. What was left was for three men to discern what God wanted, together. Paul stood up. He was the man with the facts. He talked about how Gentiles had converted enthusiastically. Peter stood up. He was the man with the vision, and told of his dream experience. Finally James stood up. He was the man with the Bible knowledge, and showed, by going through the Old Testament, how it was the original intention of God to bring the Gentiles into the fold. Three men. Three different reasons. And all together, the voice of God was discerned.

The point is, they decided it as well as God. Jesus didn't just come and hijack the meeting. And this is how the whole world works. Charles Kingsley was a clergyman utterly unfazed by Darwin's theory of evolution, which was widely viewed among people of faith as a theory that debunked the agency of God. He said that although God could have snapped the divine fingers and brought into being a ready-made world, he opted to do something far cleverer, to make a world in which creatures could 'make themselves'. That's the theological heart of evolution. God whispers because he doesn't want to be a puppet-master who has to pull every string; he whispers because he wants us to pull the strings together with him. It's like this: he whispers because *he wants to give us the chance to do the impossible in his strength*!

So when we think about all our voices, in practice maybe we should not hanker for an audible voice from God. Most of the voices we are going to have to deal with will come from 'ourselves to ourselves'. Tuning in to the Divine Voice will cost us a lot, but when we do, we find a new integrating centre that turns some voices off in their nefarious influence, and in other voices reverses their negative polarity and helps us find a way forward. If Jesus didn't hanker after an audible experience of God's voice, neither should we. If it comes, good and well. But God whispers for a reason. A very good reason. He whispers to make us pay attention and, in paying attention, find a new path and a real fullness – one that we played our part in creating.

Are there distinct voices from the pit? There must be. There is enough in the Gospels to say that there is the demonic call. Jesus refutes them in the desert. Jesus hears them when he casts out demons. Indeed, when Peter rebukes him for talking of the cross as a means to glory, Jesus is moved to call that a satanic voice. The devil – whether you take him literally or not – is any force that wants to deflect us from our divine purpose. From his point of view, voices are very useful, because he can use them without it looking like it's him. He's much more effective in disguise. Of the three images we have of him in the New Testament, two are subtle – cunning serpent, angel of light. It is to his advantage that he uses our voices. But whether a person or not, evil in this world consists of *seeking to ensure that your voices stop you presenting yourself to God.*

In practice, maybe it is not so vital to worry about whether a voice is divine or demonic in its origin. It is more important to consider a voice in terms of its effect. By tackling these two discernment questions we might be able to see if a voice is divine or malign: Is this going to help or hinder us showing up to the present moment? And, is it going to help or hinder us presenting 'all that is within us' to our Creator?

That is not as hard as it sounds!

In the last analysis, our voices start out attacking us; they are out to destroy us and atomise our deeper self. But the

Divine Voice reverses the flow. The voices that attack now help us build. God centres us. He becomes the source and help, and from this our voices serve us rather than subvert us in becoming a unique being in this wonderful garden we call the world.

If we listen to the Divine Voice – through stillness and suffering – these very voices, instead of attacking us, can serve us.

That's the process.

Lean into it.

It will save your life.

No, it will ensure that you live your life the way God intended.

He's involved.

That we may be alive.

And free.

And full.

13

Voices and World-Changing

ONE OF THE twentieth century's great architects of political revolution was L. K. Advani, who was a leader of the BJP (the Bharatiya Janata Party, translated as the Indian People's Party). He was the strategist of *Hindutva*, or Hindu extremism, a form of religious nationalism that swept into power in the late 1990s in India, even though at the beginning of the decade they could barely muster a handful of seats in the national parliament. As soon as they gained power, they were swift to target Muslim and Christian minorities with waves of violence that have only increased since the election of Narendra Modi in 2014. In the world's largest democracy, an extremist party took power fair and square, rising from discredited obscurity to form a powerful government in less than eight years.

How did he manage it? I interviewed one of Advani's inner circle at the time about how Hindu extremism got going. He said, 'Well, I looked first to see who was successful at cultural influencing and copied them.'

'Who were they?' I asked.

'The Christians,' he said. He must have seen my open mouth because he hastened to explain. 'Yes, they exert amazing influence in India quite beyond their size. They are only 2.3 per cent of the population, but they run 70 per cent of the hospitals and maybe 80 per cent of all the schools, and for years have trained virtually all the elite that run India.' Advani knew first hand. He was schooled by the Jesuits.

'What was it about them that made them so influential?' I asked.

'Because they were one,' he answered with a smile. I must have given him the open mouth again. 'They have one God – we have 33 million, and rising; they have one Scripture, the Bible – we have Scriptures so long it would take a lifetime just to read them; and they have one Church' (I don't think he looked too closely) 'whereas we had hundreds of groups and organisations.'

So Advani set out to copy these elements. Out of the pantheon of Hindu deities Ram was selected; out of all the Scriptures the Bhagavad Gita was given pre-eminence, and he began to unite the disparate elements of Hindu extremism into a disciplined unity.

'Did that do it?' I asked, and what he admitted next has stayed with me ever since.

'Oh no,' he said. 'That was all preamble to the main tactic . . . *we had to place a new voice into the head of every Hindu in India.*'

At that point he grew reticent, but the outlines of how he managed it can be easily discerned. The voice essentially was: 'Foreign religions are out to undermine our beloved Hindu heritage, and if we do not act swiftly, the India we love will be lost.' Underpinning that was a host of smaller voices. One of Advani's early tactics was to dress up a Toyota Land Cruiser in the guise of an ancient chariot and cruise around the country holding rallies, claiming that most mosques and churches were built illegitimately on the sites of the birthplaces of Hindu deities. His target was to whip mobs into frenzies and foment communal violence. This culminated in the violent demolition of the Babri mosque in the city of Ayodhya in December 1992, by a Hindu mob. Lies were used. At his rallies Advani said that the Christians were a front for the CIA, and that the Roman Catholic Church was seeking to take over India through Sonia Ghandi, the Italian-born wife of assassinated prime minister Rajiv Ghandi. Never short of an incendiary epigram, he thundered: 'We want Raj rule, not Rome rule.' Others came into his wake to bolster this dominant voice, claiming that every act of conversion away from Hinduism was always the result of unethical inducements. In less than a decade, the cultural landscape had shifted. As a Delhi pastor told me in 2000, 'Ten years ago Christians were regarded as good for society, now everyone looks at me as if I am a foreign interloper wanting to bribe Hindus away from their faith.'

Advani's strategy paid off. Of course, there was a lot more to it. Moderates failed to curb corruption and people gave up on less extremist solutions; the economy stagnated and the BJP promised the business elites a fresh approach. But in the end, Advani succeeded in implanting a *new voice* into large numbers of the Hindu majority, that their culture was under attack and they should pay any price to protect it, even if that meant suppressing the rights of minorities and betraying India's constitutional pluralism. India is a changed country today from twenty years ago because a *new voice* was deliberately inserted at the cultural level.

It's worth drawing attention to this in case we get the impression that voices only operate at an individual level and are only to do with the progress of our own souls. Voices are also articulated at a cultural level and taken down into the heart, often for worse rather than better, and this can alter societal balances and turn a culture hostile to some beliefs where it was once hospitable to them. Some voices need to be engaged at the cultural level, lest they change our own culture without us even being aware of it.

A few years ago the ministry Open Doors – the world's largest agency assisting persecuted Christians – asked persecuted leaders what the defining 'voice' was that had been introduced into their cultures that was driving much of their persecution. They came up with four global lies.

In the Middle East, the lie is that 'Christianity is a foreign religion, a Trojan horse for pro-Israel, pro-American forces'. In countries such as Egypt, and in the Palestinian Authorities, Christian leaders feel it is necessary to be extra forceful in their condemnation of Israel and the United States, because, as one Coptic bishop put it, 'Otherwise they will think we are anti-Muslim.' Yet this is the very soil in which Christianity was born and first flourished.

In the Asian subcontinent, the lie is that 'Christianity only grows through unethical or forced conversion, and wants to take over our countries by stealth'. This is the cry of the Hindu extremist in India and the Buddhist nationalist in Sri Lanka. But the fact is that it is Christianity's growth among the poorest segments of the population that threatens the extremist agenda. In India, for example, over 60 per cent of the 60 million Christian population has come from the so called 'Dalit' community, the low caste and untouchables, who must do the dirty jobs in society that the high-caste groups cannot do, lest the system collapse. It is easier to claim that these groups have been tempted away 'unethically' than to admit that a rival religion empowers the poor better.

In those countries where the Marxist ideology still lingers, such as China, North Korea, Vietnam and parts of Latin America and Africa, the lie remains this: 'Christianity is for weaklings who can't face the world on its own terms, and need crutches of illusion to get by.' In a country like China, for example, this can manifest in a government fear of organised house groups in the countryside because, as one official was overheard to say, 'The peasants will harm themselves and create social instability through foolish messiah-seeking.' In reality, those who turn to Christianity in totalitarian societies show great strength in confronting a hostile government, thus giving the lie to the 'weakling idea'.

In the West, the lie is that 'Christianity is intolerant, anti-scientific, and best kept out of public life completely'. Most often perpetrated by a secularist elite, the concern is that Christianity entails sub-rational belief in absolute categories, resulting in an anti-liberal bigotry that is subversive of the essential nature of democracy. The view is an essential misunderstanding of the history of democracy and of the nature of belief. Democracy never initially excluded religious viewpoints from public discourse, but welcomed their role in forming moral codes. And all beliefs, of whatever hue, find expression in behaviour, so to outlaw Christianity in public life is to allow only atheistic views to flourish publicly – a stealth move of staggering intolerance.

There is no doubt that the price of being a persecuted Christian is to feel that the only relationship to be had with culture is oppositional or confrontational, and we know from the wider Church that not all cultures are full of voices that are lies. Still, all we are doing here is to make the point that voices operate at a macro as well as a micro level. It would be a wise Christian who tunes in to the dominant voices of their own culture, which could operate in just the same way as we have been examining – as identity stealers. Identity wars are just another part of culture wars.

Cultural voices are deliberately planted. It still goes on. I once talked to a minister who was in charge of propaganda in an Eastern European state, and he talked of two mechanisms that embedded a cultural voice in the hearts of enough people to create change. The first was what he called the principle of ubiquity: 'A voice has to be the air you breathe, you cannot avoid it, it comes in from everywhere so that it seeps into your very being, in ways that are too numerous to police and fight off.' So they organised all platforms of the media, education, entertainment, and employment to create this total reinforcement, which of course is easier in totalitarian societies. The second was what he termed the principle of compromise: situations had to be engineered where people had to assent to the dominant voice even if they didn't believe it. That way they were compromised into obedience. This might be where they have to pass an exam affirming they are atheists in order to join the Communist Party in China today, otherwise the best jobs are barred to them. The voice requires obedience, and strangely it's more powerful if it is coerced.

But what are these voices that are out to steal our identity and that hide in the culture at large? I awoke to some possibilities while reading an old book by a long-departed theologian, H. H. Farmer. His book was called *The World and God: A Study of Prayer, Providence and Miracle in Christian Experience*, and his main point was that we have more trouble now relating to God as a person because modern life has depersonalised us. We have been shrunk in four ways by these dominant cultural voices.

Our first shrinkage is *to a machine*. This is the legacy of the Industrial Age, where we are valued purely for our labour. Since he was writing in 1935, Farmer was talking about the dehumanisation of factory life, still a fearful reality in the shirt factories of Bangladesh or the shoe factories in China. The modern economy has moved on a little to also value us purely for our intellectual activities, our creative labour in the service sector. Still, the same terrifying voice is out to steal our identity – 'You can only be happy if you are productive.' It's a tough world. You may be productive today, but what about tomorrow? Your selling numbers might be up there on the board this month. But what about next month? This voice is reducing our identity down to what we are paid to do, and we lose our anchorage in who we are before God and others.

Our second shrinkage is *to an individual*. Modern life has de-socialised us, ripping us away from the ties that bind. We are an individual where we were once a tribe, or a family. Of course, much of this individualism is liberating, and it is a beautiful thing not to have to do what our parents did, or follow their beliefs for fear of estrangement or worse. But we are on our own a lot more. We stand alone. Social ties have been seriously weakened. Families have shrunk in size and significance. Voluntary organisations have fewer members. Loneliness may be the besetting issue of the age. And the voice that comes with this is, 'It's all about you,' or, 'You have to take charge of your own wellbeing – no one else will.' But the world does not reduce to our problems, or our wellbeing. As Christians, for example, it is disastrous to shrink God down to our own experience of God. We have to inhabit our contemporary community's experience of him, the Church's experience of God over time, and even access Christ's experience of God, as well as accessing our own. Any good psalm contains a celebration of all these four dimensions of spiritual experience, and we are swept up into a great cosmic belonging. We are not meant to be lonely pilgrims. Even hermits exist in monasteries.

Our third shrinkage is *to a number*. This is the market. We are part of a market process that we cannot control and that controls us, making us a pure consumer. Even in banks today we are increasingly processed by machines that ask us for PIN numbers. The world is getting a lot less personal. Our data trail on the internet is tracked by Silicon Valley behemoths and sold to advertisers who market products to us. We are profiled by mathematical algorithms. Even charities, if they want to raise funds, must run numbers and predict with a spurious certainty empirical impacts. 'You are a series of numbers,' says this voice, 'and the question is, can you afford to be a good consumer? If not, better try harder.' The identity stealth is obvious – we are being shrunk to a consumer, which is tragic, because what we really want is always out of reach – but that's capitalism!

The fourth shrinkage of modern life is *to a heap of atoms*. This is the doing of science, which has impressed upon us our colossal insignificance in the world we live in. Much of this is very useful, of course. The British astronomer Martin Rees once worked out that if you take the expected timescale of our planet from big bang to final fizzle, and compress it into a calendar year, then the twenty-first century would be the equivalent of a quarter of a second in June. That puts us in our place. Our lives do not matter cosmically. And science has been humbling us since it began, at least in its Western incarnation. As Oxford philosopher Luciano Floridi says,

> We are no longer at the centre of the universe – thanks to Copernicus.
> We are no longer at the centre of the biological kingdom – thanks to Darwin.
> We are no longer at the centre of the realm of rationality – thanks to Freud.
> Now, we are no longer at the centre of the infosphere – thanks to Turing.

Floridi invites us to put ourselves at the *service* of the universe now that we are no longer at the *centre* of it. Fair point, but the issue of crushing insignificance cannot be overlooked so cheerfully. The danger of science is in its reductionism, at least in its naive form – we are gleefully told by some that we are nothing but a handful of atoms. We have a defining voice in the culture which pretends that a physical description of the universe is exhaustive of its reality, or if not exhaustive, the only one that can be trusted. The voice resulting is, 'Your life does not matter . . . you will soon be dead; only your atoms will go on.' Or, 'All that matters is to explain the physical . . . anything else is of no importance.' Or, in the voice of the blues song, 'You only live but once so let the good times roll.' Some may find that voice comforting of course, but if you believe we are specks of dust fused to shards of eternity, the shrinkage is disastrous, and the loss to ethics and responsibility catastrophic.

At any rate, thanks to this comprehensive dehumanisation of these voices, our capacity to relate to God as a person is fatally undermined, said H. H. Farmer in 1935, and the elements of Christianity are becoming increasingly strange to us. How should we fight back?

We need the five stratagems at this level too, though since these macro voices come from a culture that defines us, we might best respond by subsisting inside a counter-culture that gives us an alternative world. The Church comes to mind as a primary provider of this counter-culture. I have an African-American friend in Los Angeles who has experienced more than his fair share of racial discrimination, and he goes along to church purely, he says, 'To hear another voice to the one that is more appealing'. That appealing voice is to take violent action against whites and avenge the discrimination he has felt so painfully. But he admits, 'I go to church to hear the same voice as my grandmothers . . . I need the preacher to keep telling me that I can't glorify God with a gun in my hand.'

I suspect, though, that people are finding that it is not the institutional Church that contains this counter-culture. Those kinds of churches are desperate to find insertion points into an increasingly secularised society – a tough ask if your church is so preoccupied with its own stuff it barely notices the spiritual search of the culture itself. Maybe the key is to *value the prophets*. There are prophets in our society who expose its lies. They may not be religious at all. I find that much (though not all) of the critiques of intellectuals like the linguist Noam Chomsky, or the novelist Tom Wolfe, or the economist Ha-Joon Chang, are brilliant at locating me in the world with its competing voices. Or it may be a group of bloggers, unconnected with the world of academia or published success. Then, after we have found a way to see the voices unmasked, perhaps the next stage is to *find a tribe*. A group of like-minded friends and strangers who can keep us relatively immune to the clamour of the culture's voices. We can fight back if we value our prophets and find a tribe.

But it is not just prophets and tribes. We can still make a difference to these dominant cultural voices at the micro level. Megatrend watchers tell us that one of the greatest issues threatening the world today is 'global-tribalism', the paradox that the more we open up to other cultures, especially through trade (globalisation), the more defensive we become of our own (tribalism). We have rarely seen a period when polarisation has become so common or so prominent as in the politics of twenty-first-century countries. But how would we ever work to bring a new coherence? The problem seems insurmountable.

Yet all we have talked about in this book essentially gives us the capacity to reverse the polarisation that surrounds us. What drives polarisation is quite simply a refusal to listen to anyone who thinks and acts differently to us. We cannot think outside the tribe. Yet if we can learn to listen to our voices, we have actually created the capacity to listen to the voices of others, and with the same compassion that we bring to ourselves.

Only an empathic appreciation of 'the other' will save us today, and managing our voices gives us the ability – under God – to muster that appreciation. Social psychologists have pointed out what happens to us when we feel threatened by another group. We experience *cognitive constriction*, and go into the automatic defensive stratagems of fight, flight, freeze, flock or fawn. But with the ability to pause, get our breathing under control, and stop the voice creating that automatic reaction of anger and exclusion, we can get past the constriction that escalates the conflict rather than reduces it. Another way we perpetuate conflict when threatened is by exhibiting what is called *value monism*. That is where we stress a single value, say freedom of expression, over any other, especially against another group that stresses another value, say belonging. The solution is to hold values in tension, to accept that we need to value complexity, and again, this can be achieved if we are able to accept that our selves are split, and needing to be integrated by the Divine Voice. We can find the compassion to step into the shoes of the enemy, and love them.

If we cannot cross divides, and work with others from other tribes, our societies will tribalise even more. There are plenty of unscrupulous politicians like Advani who are banking on it, and working towards it.

Shall they win?

Or will we stop them planting their 'voices' into the heart of cultures, so that they seep down in the heart of each of us?

Will we go back to Babel, and be stuck in societies stymied by the mutual incomprehension of competing voices?

Or will we accept that Pentecost has happened. A new way has been given to us to turn the voices from a destructive babble into a beautiful symphony!

Take the adventure. Don't let the refusal voice at Pentecost have the final say: 'They are drunk, that's all,' and walk away. Let the wonder voice out to play: 'How can this be?'

Only in this way can the world be cured a little of its destructive polarisations, and us too, of our besetting voices of anxiety or achievement.

A better life and world awaits . . . if we can turn up to it!

Acknowledgements

SPECIAL THANKS TO my editor Katherine Venn who coaxed this book out of me when I had long moved on. Thanks also to Jessica Lacey for her excellent editing. To Andrea Wigglesworth, who first asked me to teach about Voices at the Vital Connexions Summer School at Crieff Hydro, Perthshire, in 2011. She started the ball rolling and gave great feedback. My wife Eolene co-taught that course with me, and it was the stronger for it as she brought her psychological learning into the mix. Unfortunately she was unavailable to write or shape this manuscript, but she has been a great interlocutor for me over the years on this topic. To my dear friend Nick Page, who made a way for me to meet up with Katherine and whose witty writing style I wish I could even part emulate.

I must make it clear that this is a first attempt at a subject that gets treated very little in the Christian sphere, and it shows. In addition, the book was written at high speed over five weeks. Consequently there may be much in it that is not phrased as well as it should be, and contains concepts yet to crystalize into something more refined and nuanced. The importance of the subject led me to follow the dictum of G.K. Chesterton – which explains his vast and uneven corpus – that if a thing is worth doing its worth doing badly.

I freely admit that much of what I have written is less than original, and I am delighted to give some pointers to thinkers and resources far better than I. Some will detect the influence of Princeton Practical Theologian James E Loder, whose book *The Transforming Moment* made such an impact on me. The thought of Thomas Keating and Basil Pennington (the latter who taught me contemplative prayer in Hong Kong) has been critical, and also the insights of two distinguished Ignatian Spiritual Directors under whom I was privileged to make a number of retreats – Bill Broderick and Gerard Hughes. All – with the exception of Bill – have written books that shaped me and are wonderfully profitable to read, and better than mine. If my book can help you to read theirs, my job is done.

HODDER &
STOUGHTON

Hodder & Stoughton is the UK's
leading Christian publisher,
with a wide range of books from
the bestselling authors in the UK
and around the world ranging from
Christian lifestyle and theology to
apologetics, testimony and fiction.
We also publish the world's
most popular Bible translation
in modern English, the New
International Version, renowned
for its accuracy and readability.

Hodderfaith.com   Hodderbibles.co.uk
@HodderFaith   /HodderFaith